# Philosophy of Religion

## AN INTRODUCTION

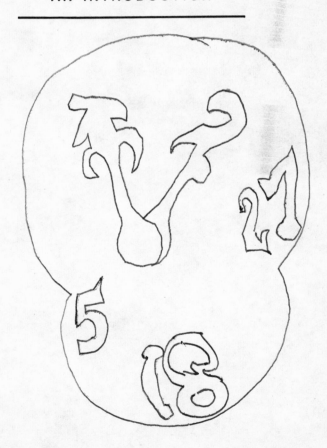

# Philosophy of Religion
## AN INTRODUCTION

## William H. Capitan

**PEGASUS**

A DIVISION OF

THE BOBBS-MERRILL COMPANY, INC., PUBLISHERS

Indianapolis                    New York

This book is one of series, Traditions in Philosophy, published in cooperation with Educational Resources Corporation, which created and developed the series under the direction of Nicholas Capaldi, Professor of Philosophy, Queens College, New York.

For a Good Shepherd

# Acknowledgments

The author is grateful to the following for permission to reprint: From *A Confession; The Gospel in Brief; What I Believe; Ivan Ilych; Hadji Murad and Other Stories* by Leo Tolstoy, translated by Louise and Aylmer Maude: Oxford University Press.

From Søren Kierkegaard, *Concluding Unscientific Postscript,* translated by David F. Swenson and Walter Lowrie (copyright 1941, 1969 by Princeton University Press; Princeton Paperback, 1968), pp. 178, 182, 189, and 220. Reprinted by permission of Princeton University Press and The American Scandinavian Foundation.

From Philostratus, *Life of Apollonius of Tyana,* Volume 1: The Loeb Classical Library and Harvard University Press.

From The Revised Standard Version of the Bible, © 1946 and 1952, used by permission: National Council of the Churches of Christ.

From *Three Philosophical Poets* by George Santayana: Harvard University Press.

From *The Brothers Karamazov* by Fyodor Dostoevsky, translated by Constance Garnett: Random House, Inc.

From John Hick: *Faith and Knowledge.* First edition © 1957, second edition © 1966 by Cornell University Press. Used by permission of Cornell University Press.

# Contents

# Preface

This book is for students and general readers. It covers only some of the many topics in philosophy of religion, but those it covers might interest especially the person who thinks about religion today. The variety of topics discussed is broad enough to give the reader an understanding of the richness of the field, and the topics are treated in sufficient detail to acquaint the reader with one typical approach to philosophy of religion. The historical contexts and the historical order in which the topics appear should help the reader to gain a proper perspective on the philosophical status of religion in the present age, removing both deceptive props of religious belief and unnecessary obstacles to religious belief. The biggest problem facing the person interested in religion is the lack of attention given to it. I hope this book will help in some way to show how serious the philosophical questions about religion are.

Many thanks are due to many people. R. G. Collingwood has been an unfailing philosophical source, and my interest in religion has been sustained by my knowing that religion occupied the attention of this great philosopher throughout his lifetime. I owe much to my students and colleagues at Oberlin College, especially my friend and colleague Daniel Merrill, who kindly read and commented on the whole manuscript. Nicholas Capaldi, the editor of this series, has been extremely patient and helpful. I am grateful to Mrs. Betty Wigginton, whose enthusiasm and interest in the book helped steer us through many technicalities. Besides typing the manuscript, she served as my model general reader.

# I

# Introduction

Men today find it difficult to believe anything about the universe, or even man himself, unless it comes from the sciences. Scientific discoveries about man and the world appear to challenge what religions typically offer—significance to man's existence. Some men even fear that religious beliefs cannot withstand philosophical scrutiny because they will be found inconsistent with scientifically established facts.

This attitude toward religious belief has not always existed. Among certain scholastic thinkers, philosophy was the handmaiden of theology, not the mother of the sciences. This book traces the decline of the scholastic view of philosophy and the rise of the modern view, but at the same time takes philosophy as primary. It views philosophy as rational inquiry into the structure of any thought system, its presuppositions, concepts, and the status of its claims.

We shall see some theologians challenging even this status of philosophy. They will contend that philosophy cannot stand above all disciplines as pure rational inquiry because it cannot proceed without holding beliefs no more scientifically grounded than those said to rest on faith. So we must beware of the idea that philosophy is merely an examination of the truths and procedures of other disciplines, helpful though this model of it may be in the early stages of our work.

Moreover, religion is not in any ordinary sense a mere thought system and is called one only by ignoring its important aspects. Theology is a proper thought system because it treats of God in accordance with the canons of reason. It was even called a science in the days before science appropriated the term for itself. Religion, by contrast, is better viewed as something lived and believed rather than as mere thought, even though it involves thought. Religious people profess beliefs, but they also perform rituals, pray, meditate, worship, have meetings, and keep holy days. The philosopher must translate these activities into a rationally manageable form, whatever that might be. Many thinkers claim this cannot be done, and some say it cannot even be partly done.

This raises doubts about our being able to say what specifically we are talking about when we talk of religion, and whether it is correct to talk of religion in a general sense rather than to talk of the different religions we know from the works of historians and anthropologists. For example, the philosopher cannot reflect on all religion merely by examining the proposition that God exists. Some religions do not involve that claim at all. Even focusing on one religion is complicated because religions seem to change throughout history. The difference between primitive Christianity and modern Christianity, for example, is striking.

Christians have taken elaborate measures to preserve the continuity of their experience in the creeds and through official promulgators of doctrine; and as a result the complex experience of being a Christian has changed less than it might have. But we should not underestimate the impact of purely secular developments on this experience. The amount God is alleged to act in the universe has decreased from earlier days, when it was assumed that God not only created the universe but also sustained it and frequently became manifest in it. Modern Christians might well wonder whether the claim "God acts" has any meaning at all. This change is investigated in the following chapters.

Also, some philosophers believe that the very concept of religion is open-textured—meaning that religion has no terminable list of defining qualities because religions change, as we have seen, and because they share a considerable yet indeterminable number of characteristics with activities we would not ordinarily think of as religions. So these philosophers conclude that it is pointless to talk of religion and necessary to examine religions individually and descriptively.

This is worth remembering as we cover the topics in this book. But the important question about religion today is, not so much which religion one will accept, but whether he will accept any at all—whether any religion offers a tenable view of man and the world, and whether a viable way of life follows from it.

The question for philosophy becomes, What is the difference between the religious and the secular views of the world and their implied ways of life? This does not make all religions alike, nor does it yield the essence of religion; but it does show where philosophy of religion for the modern reader should focus. Differences among religions, except as they bear upon this point, may be left aside.

Besides, it may still be worth talking of religion as such. Too often the differences among religions are cited from fossilized descriptions of religions, listing features of religions such as whether they include a god, prayer, or immortality, and in general comparing them to Christian belief. And the overlap of religious with other human activities becomes problematic only if one thinks the religious material of philosophy appears nowhere but in traditionally recognized religions; this is like thinking art appears only in art museums and nowhere else.

With these considerations in mind—and some others to appear later—I have devised the strategy of this book. Basically, the book follows a broad historical path. This has the advantage of making philosophical biases less important, and the added advantage that historical organization is familiar to most readers. Also, this form should make more obvious the changes in the relationship between philosophy and religion, the impact of science on religion, and the development of the modern predicament of religion.

The book is historical in another sense. Each chapter includes classical sources of the topics discussed. This is important for those who plan to read more philosophy, more theology, and more about religion, since the sources are the common frames of reference in the literature of these fields.

Finally, the book does not cover all topics in philosophy of religion—if there is any meaningful sense to "all" here —but it does cover enough topics for the reader to enter well into the subject. It plunges in *medias res,* without a great deal of preliminary definition, as the best way to initiate the new philosopher of religion. This way he will be able to think more clearly about the subject than had he learned a battery of definitions *in vacuo.* Even the essential mapping is better done by the reader himself, based on the clarification of his own thought. This book seeks to lead him in that direction by historical illustration of a variety of views and debates on key topics.

## Traditional Theism.

To trace the evolution of thought culminating in the modern religious situation, one must begin with traditional theism. Theism is belief in one God—in the world but also beyond it, therefore not identical to it, although he acts in it. Stated technically, for traditional theism God is both transcendent and immanent. The Judeo-Christian idea of God is theistic because God has created the world and so affects it, yet is decidedly distinct from it.

There are other attributes given to God by the Judeo-Christian theist. To understand these attributes, and the belief in a being who has them, an examination of one of the so-called proofs for the existence of God will help. It will show that not just any argument with the conclusion "God exists" will do. The subject of the conclusion must fit with one's religious beliefs. For example, one might conclude "God exists" by defining "God" to be equivalent to some well-established natural phenomenon —love, say, or even the natural world. But this does not prove that the Judeo-Christian God exists. And this shows that the being to be proven to exist is not altogether elusive. There is a traditional conception of God, though it is difficult to put in convenient logical form and is the subject of debate among theologians.

**The Teleological Argument** is one of several arguments for the existence of God. There is not space to consider other arguments in their historical contexts and thus do them justice, so we shall confine our attention to just this one. It still has a certain *prima facie* appeal which the others have lost with time. The teleological argument has many variations and degrees of refinement. The premises vary from primitive responses to weather, to sophisticated scientific observations. In the age of its greatest use Newton had taught men to view the world as an intricately ordered whole, intelligible through the laws governing its workings.

So the argument would go like this:

1.  The world is throughout marked by order.
2.  This order cannot arise by chance.
3.  Therefore, there must be a creator of this order.

Cast in this way the argument turns on the design which

implies a designer, hence the name "argument from design." It could be cast by saying that the world exists for the sake of an end, and so be called the teleological argument. This would require pointing out that end in the basic premise, but what that end is would be determined by reflection on the nature of the alleged design.

To infer this, however, more is required. We have to be able to draw upon our experience of designs and their designers, and then compare these familiar designs with the entire universe. Then we can infer by analogy what the designer of the universe must be like. A version of the teleological argument so expressed as to reveal this aspect of the reasoning is called "argument from analogy." Because of the intimate connection of all three aspects— teleology, design, and analogy—the same basic argument goes under these names. Which name a philosopher uses depends on which aspect he is contemplating.

This argument is not difficult to understand because its major premise is obviously true and its minor premise is intuitive. It suggests the idea of Providence, a standard idea in Western religions. It also seems to simplify inferences about God's nature. Whoever created such a magnificent machine must be superbly intelligent and incomprehensibly powerful. Of the traditional characteristics of God, only his benevolence does not follow simply. But the visible order suggests the world was not an accident, and man's place in it seems a happy one. So this reasoning is quite consonant with traditional religion.

Moreover, the argument allegedly rests on scientific observation in such a way that new scientific discoveries will not detract but add to its claim of order, just as they will add to God's majesty. New discoveries will be further revelation of God's power and intellect. And God's benevolence will be witnessed by the discoveries of order suiting each sentient creature to its place in creation.

Indeed, certain thinkers of the seventeenth and eighteenth centuries said this way of thinking was natural to man and his entire religion could rest upon this foundation. These thinkers were called deists. Their religion was called natural religion. They thought they could even dismiss the vagaries and superstitutions of holy scripture.

They did this at considerable cost, however. They emphasized order in the world to where it seemed offensive to think of God's entering it to act. Any such act of God would be trifling with a marvelous plan. What happens in the world happens because of the laws according to which everything must happen. Signs, wonders, and miracles have no place in the world. This is why in modern usage deism is belief in a god who created the world but who does not act in it.

Thus we can see already how the type of argument one would use implied his special conception of God. But let us pursue the argument further by seeing how David Hume (1711–76) criticizes it in his *Dialogues Concerning Natural Religion* and how William Paley (1743–1805) defends it.

First, Hume objects that the argument is not a very good specimen of argument from analogy. In arguments of this sort a perfect similarity of cases gives us assurance as strong as anything in experience, but the least departure from perfect similarity renders the argument proportionately weaker. For example, when we have witnessed the circulation of blood in human beings, we do not doubt that it is the same with any other human being. But when we have witnessed it in only frogs and fishes, we are not entitled to a strong presumption that by analogy it occurs in men and other animals. And our analogical reasoning would be very much weaker should we infer from blood circulation in animals to sap circulation in plants. Now think how very different the entire universe is from any one thing in it.

Second, if the only way we can determine what has caused something is by experience, then clearly we are in no position to infer anything about the cause of the universe.

We have not experienced the creation of a universe. The order we see in the world does not reveal itself as the result of design. We have to have seen that this kind of order is in fact the result of design before we can infer a designer.

Third, given the first two objections, any inference to a designer merely from the fact of order must rest on the dubious assumption that a designing intelligence is the only possible source of order. But this must be established. There are many ways to account for order. Indeed, matter may have its own principle of order just as the mind does. Unless self-ordering is at some point possible, then a quest for the world-ordering principle in a designing mind would send us on an infinite journey looking for another mind in which ideas ordered themselves. Holding this much, we may as well hold that nature contains her own source of order. It was the implicit denial that there could be self-ordering that set us off in search of a designing intelligence in the first place.

These objections emphasize our ignorance of the origin of the world and our inability to transfer what we know from living in the world to the mystery of the origin of the world. But, in addition to our lack of knowledge, there is also an inherent limitation upon what we can reason effectively about and how we can manage the information we do have. Hume points out that in those things we are competent to think about, we can confidently work to some one answer which is more or less convincing. But in the ultimate questions traditionally found in religion, there is room for an enormous amount of fact-juggling to make an analogy seem to work. The odds are "a thousand, a million to one, if either yours or any one of mine be the true system." [1]

William Paley argued against Hume. Paley believed that there is something special about the order we live in and see around us. It will be well to look at Paley's reasoning since many people regard Hume as having finished the business long before Paley made it the center of his *Natural Theology*.[2]

Paley argues that our experience gives clear evidence of design in nature since the analogy between many natural structures and man-made, artificial structures is clear. He draws an analogy between the human eye and a watch and argues that we see in both the integration of working parts and their integration for the sake of a certain result. This alone allows us to infer that they are designed and *must* have had a designer.

Paley argues, against Hume's causal objection, that it is not necessary to observe the design being carried out in something in order to know it is designed. Something could even be designed by superhuman intelligence and we could still tell it was designed and not accidental.

Paley argues, against Hume's self-ordering-of-matter objection, that it is doubtful a principle of order is ultimately different from an intelligent creator. To speak of order is to speak of the adaptation of means to an end, and this means that one is speaking of intention. It is difficult to see how one can do that without referring to some mind or other.

Paley argues, above all, order does not pervade the whole universe, anyway—at least, not the order he has in mind. Paley has in mind the special adaptations of living organisms to their environment, clear individual cases. We may know very little about the whole universe just as Hume says, but we do know of special cases in which there must have been a designer, and from this we can infer directly the existence of a designer.

Is Paley convincing? It seems that his reasoning would entitle him to infer only a designer of the order he cites, not a designer of the total universe. But this would seem to be all that Paley needs. Any individual case of design completely inexplicable without reference to a designer would be a beginning for Paley. He could then gather data which fit with his hypothesis that there is design throughout the universe.

It is not easy to say what makes such inferences possible, but it is certain that we make them and that a substantial part of our knowledge rests on them. I have in mind our knowledge of certain human behavior, certain integrations and arrangements of bodily movements, which we take as knowledge of intelligent action.[3] Just so, we infer intelligence from design in nature. And this is possible whether or not we can know the origins of whatever we are investigating.

This is behind Paley's reply to Hume, and this is why Paley would reject the modern version of Hume's point by John Wisdom in his article, "Gods." [4] There Wisdom says we are as wanderers in a wilderness who chance upon a formation in the vegetation suggesting to us the work of a gardener whose existence we cannot in any way detect unless the formation justifies inference to him. We might say "A garden!" but we might equally say "An accidental formation in the jungle resembling a garden!" This is where Paley stands firm.

Paley will not agree that the formations are like that. All of his considerations disallow this, not merely by making an accidental formation improbable, but also by showing that the phenomenon in question comes from design by all of the criteria we have which enable us to judge something to be the result of intelligent design. Of course, this does not exclude utterly the possibility that we are mistaken about what the formation indicates. Paley writes at times as if he is aware of this point. But he thinks we are *as* justified in inferring a designer as we are in inferring that a certain polished stone is a sculpture and not merely a stone washed by the surf.

Here we should pause. It seems that sometimes things look carefully planned but are really accidental. We find ourselves forced to consider the conditions of origin in order to decide. Paley denies this. Wisdom seems to consider the matter a mere turn of mind. And just here Hume, the skeptic, claims his triumph: We cannot know because we cannot go outside or beyond the system within which we find the order to resolve our differences. The inference to a designer is not false but unwarranted. And this is no less true of individual things than of the entire universe. Some-one might still say that the inner character of the world system is compatible with the belief in a designer outside the system. But though this move is possible one owes us a reason for making it.

The theory of evolution, in its finer-grained description of the origins of the species, presents a picture of man in the universe suggesting thoughts profoundly incompatible with the presuppositions of theism and of a thinker like Paley. Just as the Copernican view of the solar system shattered the hierarchical view of the universe, the theory of evolution shattered the view of man as the intentional crowning achievement of Nature. The evolutionary view draws attention to the suffering and the ruthless fight for survival between man and nature and between man and man—in short, to everything the theist calls evil.

This is not to suggest that religious people are not aware of evil. As we shall see, they characteristically notice it when others tend to ignore it. But the facts brought to the fore by the new view make it difficult to believe that a benevolent deity could have planned such a drama. Even allowing that some evil is necessary for God's inscrutable ways, all the evil we see is now in such overwhelming and pointless abundance that we are forced to interpret life under the more adequate hypothesis that it was all the result of chance.

The evolutionary view of man has implications for moral theology. The theist finds in natural law something like an ideal or a prescriptive norm as well as a descriptive one, whereas the evolutionist finds only a descriptive one. For the former, man is placed in nature for his fulfill-ment and abuses natural laws at the peril of natural pain, not only in such infractions as putting one's hand in fire and having it burned, but also in his seeking to redirect or to control nature—whether performing operations on him-self from surgery to "artificial" birth control, or operations on natural processes other than his own. The latter would deny that such prescriptions are written in nature. For him man can do to himself or to the rest of nature what he will, and what consequences he has to fear are not moral but physical. Moral reflections have no place here and are of a different order entirely. Men will use their knowledge of scientific laws to promote their ends, whatever they may be.

The theist feels that man is not alone in the course of events and is limited in his capacity to foresee the full consequences of his interaction with nature. Man is not the master and should not behave as if he is. Too often he is unwilling to look beyond his own interests. Man's capacity to know is limited by his finitude, even with the best will in the world.[5] This view may not be peculiarly theistic. Anyone with good sense should know, for example, that the present generation should not live in the world as the last—that it will not be the last to use the campsite. The theist, however, is *required* to think beyond himself as part of his duty and relationship to God.

We can see some dilemmas in abandoning natural law for descriptive law. The most obvious is over man himself. If the biological description of man does not offer guidelines for behavior, then it would seem difficult to find restrictions upon man's use of technology to alter himself or his surroundings. Specifically, the increased frequency of transplants of organs taken from recently deceased or nearly deceased persons has led to attempts to redefine with greater exactness the distinction between life and death. The difficulties involved are reminiscent of those encountered by Roman Catholics who would distinguish two kinds of birth control, natural and artificial, by referring to biological processes.

This problem is beyond the scope of this book, but we should note that both theists and atheists take biological processes seriously as guides to action. The former sees them as implying restrictions safeguarding those processes and the latter sees them as suggesting ways of using our knowledge to improve life. But it is difficult to find normative suggestions in the processes themselves and to draw sharp lines certifying courses of action. And if natural laws cannot serve as ideals, then there may be no guidelines for deciding what adds or detracts from life.

### The Problem of Evil.

The presence of evil in the world poses a problem for the theist who holds that God is both omnipotent and benevolent. In the face of evil one can hold without difficulty that God is benevolent as long as he does not also try to hold that God is omnipotent or as long as he holds that God is in some way incapable of eliminating evil. Otherwise, he must hold that God for some reason allows evil. And he will be fortunate if he can show that God cannot prevent evil or, at least, only allows and does not cause it. The third alternative, believing that God does not even exist, does not interest the theist.

Hume's *Dialogues,* Part X, provides an excellent historical locus in which to study the problem of evil. It proceeds in the ambience of natural theology, is concerned with the question of God's benevolence rather than his existence, and so is a reflection on theism taken seriously. It does not seek a refutation of the claim God exists so much as it uses the fact of evil to cast doubt on our ability to know God is benevolent. Evil does not show that God does not exist, that God is not benevolent, and that God is not omnipotent. At best it can show He is not all three, and then only if there is reason to doubt there could be an explanation beyond our ability to know.

The point is not that God is malevolent, but that nature provides no basis for asserting God is benevolent, certainly not in any normal sense of that word. And unless one can believe God is benevolent in some humanly intelligible sense, there is little or no point at all in establishing God's other attributes—certainly not if our objective is to provide a ground for natural religion.[6]

To show God is benevolent we need an argument that

man, if not entirely happy, is for the most part happy. Now, no one with any experience of life will say that men are for the most part happy. And it is utterly impossible to compute all pains and pleasures and all good and evil acts of man in order to produce the estimate required to conclude that God is benevolent. A proposition of the form "Men are for the most part happy" is unquantifiable and unverifiable. If this is the required basis of natural religion, then natural religion has no foundation at all.

Even worse, nothing is gained by allowing that "Men are for the most part happy" is in some sense true. From God, as the theist understands him, we should reasonably expect no misery at all. And even allowing that evil is compatible with God's nature gains nothing. Proof of God's benevolence is still needed. Thus Hume's discussion runs.

We can now appreciate the significance of the problem of evil for theists and better assess the value, if any, of attempts to solve the problem. It is already clear that these attempts would not show from experience that God is benevolent. They can only show that one may believe, if he has other grounds, that God is omnipotent, omniscient, and benevolent too, even if evil exists. At best they will show that the traditional conception of God is coherent and consistent with the facts of experience.

It is not quite accurate, however, to leave the theist entirely on the defensive by saying that the problem of evil is his—that he must account for the natural disasters which cause incalculable suffering, anguish, and meaningless death, and that he must account for the untold wickedness of men. Some theists reply that the atheist must account for the natural events and the deeds of men which are good. The atheist may reply that neither good nor evil needs to be accounted for because it can be explained easily by reference to natural causes: earthquakes happen because of certain geological conditions and men injure each other because of certain psychological conditions.

Just here we can see that the theist is not entirely on the

defensive. The atheist refuses to account for good just as he refuses to ask for an ultimate explanation of the world. The difference, then, is that the theist is trying to take suffering and wickedness seriously rather than to avoid thinking about them. And when he does, he tries to supply an interpretation of suffering and wickedness consistent with a meaningful existence. So, in part, the issue comes down to seeing whether the theist or the atheist is dealing more responsibly with the phenomena, and I am suggesting the possibility, at least, that the theist is driven to deal with the problem of evil, not merely because of his desire to believe in God, but because of his desire to work out a world view inclusive of important facts of human life.

One of the oldest and most common attempts to deal with evil in a theistic framework is found at the beginning of the Book of Job. Suffering is God's punishment of man for his moral frailty. Job's wretchedness is presumably brought upon him for something he has done wrong. And when it comes out that Job has no sin upon him, it is suggested that there must be some sin upon him not known, perhaps not even by Job himself. Clearly, no man is morally perfect and therefore anyone is subject to God's punishment. Then, again, it may be because of guilt in the family, as when it is said that a son suffers for his father's sins.

But this reasoning only begins to deal with the evil of undeserved suffering. In effect, it denies that there is undeserved suffering by insisting that all suffering derives from sin and this justifies God's inflicting the suffering. To go further we must distinguish between two kinds of evil—moral and physical. Moral evil results from man's free will. Man can inflict suffering upon himself and others, and God is not directly responsible. Much of the evil in the world, then, is directly attributable to man. And now the question is whether the physical evil, which man does not bring about, is in any way commensurate with man's self-willed wickedness.

I believe it is not difficult to argue that the physical evil man has to suffer is far greater than any reasonable punishment his misdeeds would require. Whole cities have been destroyed by natural evils, and the worst one could say about the cities is that most of the inhabitants were wicked. Some men have had to suffer weeks, months, and even years of dreadful pain, and the worst one could say against them is that they lived unclean lives. All of this is true while many tyrants and degenerates of the lowest kind flourish and suffer nothing.

To avoid concluding we live in an unjust world, some have argued that the world must contain some suffering. Certain goods could not have been created unless evil also existed—goods we would not want to forego. For example, God created human freedom even though it entails the possibility of human error. To eliminate our capacity to err is to take away free will. This view which might include goods other than human freedom might be summarized by saying that this world contains evil but it is the best of all possible worlds. There are other possible worlds—and perhaps some without evil—but they do not contain the comparable totality of good contained in this one. Even the omnipotent God cannot create this amount of good without some evil. This view is often associated with the philosopher Leibniz (1646–1716).

Another explanation, attributable to Berkeley (1685–1753),[7] is to argue that the evil we experience is merely apparent. We assess events only from our human ends and thus call anything which frustrates our ends evil. It is not evil in any objective sense, and if we had enough perspective, we would see it contributes to the total world process and so is good. An obvious objection to this attempt is that it does not take evil seriously in the way Judaism or Christianity does. It is a complicated theological question whether these religions regard evil as the result of deliberate action by the deity (or some lesser force) or they regard evil as the result of something's going wrong.[8] But it is clear that they regard evil as real and not illusion—something man must eliminate if he can.

An obvious objection to these lines of thought is that they obscure the sense of "benevolence" we want to apply to God who made the choices which formed the world. If God's choices were not for man's happiness, then it would seem we are not much better off with this answer than we are without it. A lesser but equally obvious objection is that all of this is mere conjecture.

Probably the strongest position a theist can take on the problem of evil is to hold that God does not intend the world to be a place with human happiness as its end. Man is destined for more than a life free of suffering and the suffering of this life is a means to this end. What God has set for us is known only to him, but it will be achieved through suffering. That the world does not provide happiness for all is not, therefore, a disproof of God's benevolence. Viewed in this way the apparent unfair distribution of suffering and prosperity in this life will be set right in the future or in the present in ways unknown to us. Evil is an obstacle to religious belief only if the destiny of man is understood as the totality of undisturbed pleasures afforded by a Sunday afternoon in suburban Ohio.

Dostoevsky in *The Brothers Karamazov* presents a particularly modern reaction to this position. Ivan Karamazov tells his brother Alyosha, a novice, the following story:

One day a serf boy, a little child of eight, threw a stone in play and hurt the paw of the general's favorite hound. "Why is my favorite dog lame?" He is told that the boy threw a stone that hurt the dog's paw. "So you did it." The general looked the child up and down. "Take him." He was taken—taken from his mother and kept shut up all night. Early that morning the general comes out on horseback, with the hounds, his dependents, dog-boys, and huntsmen, all mounted around him in full hunting parade. The servants are summoned for their edification, and in front of them all stands the mother of the child. The child is brought from the lockup. It's a gloomy, cold, foggy autumn day, a capital day for hunting. The general orders the child to be undressed; the child is stripped naked. He shivers, numb with terror, not daring to cry. . . . "Make him run," commands the general. "Run! run!" shout the dog-boys. The boy runs. . . . "At him!" yells the general, and he sets the whole pack of hounds on the child. The hounds catch him, and tear him to pieces before his mother's eyes! . . . I believe the general was afterwards declared incapable of administering his estates. Well—what did he deserve? To be shot? To be shot for the satisfaction of our moral feelings? [9]

Alyosha, the monk, agrees that the general should be shot. Ivan asks,

If all must suffer to pay for the eternal harmony, what have children to do with it, tell me, please? It's beyond all comprehension why they should suffer, and why they should pay for the harmony. . . . And if it is really true that they must share responsibility for all their fathers' crimes, such a truth is not of this world and is beyond my comprehension. . . . Oh, Alyosha, I am not blaspheming! I understand, of course, what an upheaval of the universe it will be, when everything in heaven and earth blends in one hymn of praise and everything that lives and has lived cries aloud: "Thou art just, O Lord, for Thy ways are revealed." When the mother embraces the fiend who threw her child to the dogs, and all three cry aloud with tears, . . . then, of course, the crown of knowledge will be reached and all will be made clear. But what pulls me up here is that I can't accept that harmony. . . . And if the sufferings of children go to swell the sum of sufferings which was necessary to pay for truth, then I protest that the truth is not worth such a price.[10]

For the agonies of this life to be justified, they would have to serve an end so remote from human understanding that it would have no meaning for us. This is sometimes put philosophically by saying that at least part of the evil we experience is dysteleological, i.e. serving no end that could possibly justify it because there could be no such end which had any relevance to human comprehension. Ivan raises

the question whether the theist can preserve the seriousness of this world and hope for a future resolution.

This suggests a limit to theological moves made to
reconcile the ways of God to men: It is not enough to say
that God's end is a secret. It must still have meaning for us,
no matter how limited we are. If it does not, then there is
nothing to saying that God is benevolent, even *saying* it,
not proving it. It is already clear that it cannot be proved.

Another Russian writer provides us with a story suggesting that Ivan Karamazov may be too quick in deciding
when suffering is so far beyond any possible use that it
makes the cost of this world too great. In "The Death of
Ivan Ilyich" Tolstoy gives an account of the spiritual
growth of a man dying with great pain for no good reason
as the result of an injury sustained in home-decorating.
Only a few hours away from death, Ivan Ilyich, until his
accident a typical bourgeois government official, reflects as
follows:

> For three whole days, during which time did not exist for
> him, he struggled in that black sack into which he was being
> thrust by an invisible, resistless force. He struggled as a man
> condemned to death struggles in the hands of the execu-
> tioner, knowing that he cannot save himself. And every
> moment he felt that despite all his efforts he was drawing
> nearer and nearer to what terrified him. He felt that his
> agony was due to his being thrust into that black hole and
> still more to his not being able to get right into it. He was
> hindered from getting into it by his conviction that his life
> had been a good one. That very justification of his life held
> him fast and prevented his moving forward, and it caused
> him most torment of all. . . .
> And suddenly it grew clear to him that what had been
> oppressing him and would not leave him was all dropping
> away at once from two sides, from ten sides, and from all
> sides. He was sorry for them, he must act so as not to hurt
> them: release them and free himself from these sufferings.
> "How good and how simple" he thought. "And the pain?"
> he asked himself. "What has become of it? Where are you,
> pain?"

He turned his attention to it.

"Yes, here it is. Well, what of it? Let the pain be."

"And death . . . where is it?"

He sought his former accustomed fear of death and did not find it. "Where is it? What death?" There was no fear because there was no death.

In place of death there was light.

"So that's what it is!" he suddenly exclaimed aloud. "What joy!"

To him all this happened in a single instant, and the meaning of that instant did not change. For those present his agony continued for another two hours. Something rattled in his throat, his emaciated body twitched, then the gasping and rattle became less and less frequent.

"It is finished!" said someone near him.

He heard these words and repeated them in his soul.

"Death is finished," he said to himself. "It is no more!"

He drew in a breath, stopped in the midst of a sigh, stretched out, and died.[11]

Whatever its limitations because it is fiction, it makes clear how physical pain can lead to spiritual development, making pain and even death cease to be evils. And thus it eliminates some of the resistance to the theist's view by showing that what might appear useless suffering may be serving in remarkable ways. But in its way it also detracts from the theist's position on evil by suggesting the possibility of an acceptance of suffering and death apart from the hope of an eschatological rectification.

Another, more important, idea relevant to the problem of evil is the effect interpretation can have upon suffering and how the meaning of life, as it were, can supersede in importance the greatest possible pain. This may be seen in the context of T. S. Eliot's *The Cocktail Party,* where an account is given of the fate of one of the socialites, Celia Copelstone, who entered a nursing order. She joined two other sisters in a Christian village, and they had been overworked for weeks trying to heal the sick and dying. Then an insurrection broke out among the heathen. The sisters knew of it but refused to leave the dying in the village.

Two of the sisters escaped, but one of them died in the jungle, and the other can never live a normal life again. The third one was Celia. She was captured and crucified near an anthill.[12]

To those in London her death was just for a handful of plague-stricken natives who died anyway. But they did not know that two years before this she had been in a conversation in which two ways of life were distinguished for her. The first is reconciliation to the human condition wherein one maintains himself by ceasing to regret his failings and adopting the common routine. The second way is unknown and its destination cannot be described. So it requires faith of the kind that issues from despair. But when, after a blind, terrifying journey, it is reached, the same liberation from solitude and the shuffling memories and desires offered by the first way is achieved. Neither way, then, is better, but a choice must be made between them. Celia's London friends did not know she *chose* the second.

This changes the meaning of Celia's death, or so Eliot would suggest. It is not that her loneliness or her physical suffering were less, as her London friends tried to say, but that these and all other evils cease to be the central concern and begin to serve as means to the proper and highest forms of life of which humans are capable.

Ivan Karamazov seems to have realized this, but he also realizes that children make no such choice. While their suffering affects others, this unfortunately makes the children's lives into something less than ends. And Ivan feels torn between this life as an end in itself and this life as a means to a higher life. Eliot might say to him that he cannot hold this life ultimately dear unless he believes in the future harmony: this life contains such people as the insane general. That would heighten the paradox we have been witnessing in these paragraphs.

But do we have Celia's choice? If we can put this or a similar interpretation on the human condition, then evil is not that serious. Possibly a reconciliation to the human condition can be made without reference to something outside it. The drama, whether it be tragedy, comedy, or tragicomedy, has its own meaning and humans can learn to be satisfied with that even with its suffering and all. To this the theist would reply that humans may even be able to be so satisfied, but they have never been; and when they have tried, they have lapsed into the despair of meaninglessness—the shuffling memories and desires.

The question comes down to whether reconciliation to the human condition requires belief in a higher-order resolution of evil. It is here that the humanist and the theist, no matter how humanistic the latter may be, must part company. We shall explore this disagreement further after a fuller examination of the grounds of theistic belief. We shall return to it as the question of the meaning of life. I hope I have shown how pain in itself is not the ultimate constituent in the problem of evil that it has often been made out to be.

# II

## Revelation, Miracle, and Immortality

*Introduction.*

In this chapter I shall discuss three topics—revelation, miracle, and immortality. Under them fall a number of typical religious beliefs. These topics are not so closely connected with one another that they must be discussed together, and there are many ways to study each of them. But grouping them together in this way reveals connections among them which are especially interesting in the philosophical scrutiny of religion and important for religious belief. Many people believe holy scriptures are the revealed word of God, and one reason they do is that many miracles are recounted in and associated with holy scriptures.

Indeed, in one sense, revelation from God, in any form, is itself miraculous. Some forms may have a stronger suggestion of the miraculous than others. This seems to vary with a religious people's level of civilization. A familiar elementary form of revelation is the experience of possession by a god enabling a person to grasp supernatural truths which he may communicate during or after the experience. The psychological phenomena accompanying such possession are conspicuously abnormal, possibly serving in part as a sign to those in contact with the individual that he is indeed possessed and that his speech and actions are those of a god—thus presumably settling the question of authority or authenticity by direct experience.

The basic notion is that a god becomes incarnate in the body of a man, and this incarnation may be fleeting or enduring. When it is of short duration, it is called possession. Here the revelation is supernatural knowledge usually manifested in divination and prophecy. When a divine spirit remains incarnate in a human body, more than knowledge is expected—usually the performance of miracles and other wonders. When possession occurs, the human being's personality seems to disappear while the presence of the spirit shows in convulsive shiverings and shakings of the man's whole body, wild gestures, and excited looks. These are understood to be expressions, not of the man, but of the spirit which has entered him. Whatever he says in this state is accepted as the voice of the god in him and speaking through him.[1]

Others forms of revelation, associated by some scholars with more advanced religions, come to a man in trances, dreams, visions, auditions, or even from an "inner voice" much like that of one's own conscience. Inspiration, which these more sophisticated forms might more properly be called, might even be induced. The prophetess of Apollo ate the sacred laurel and was perfumed with it before she prophesied. The bacchanals ate a certain species of ivy and reached a frenzy of inspiration, possibly because of the intoxicating properties of the plant. In southern India it is believed that after the priest sucks the blood streaming from the cut throat of a goat, the goddess Kali descends upon him and he gives oracular replies.

The most refined form of revelation, associated with the most "developed" religions, is alleged to come to a person when he is in a state of heightened consciousness, neither possessed nor literally inspired, but only beyond ordinary consciousness in a state of receiving divine truths. This form is usually associated with the writing of holy scriptures; the basic notion is that a god has directed the writer in some way, and the way may be unknown even to the writer. Obviously, it is difficult—even for those inclined to accept the idea of revelation—to establish the authenticity of "revealed" scripture. The difficulty is special to this form in a way it is not to the possession form where the god's presence is supposed to be observable.

It is this third form which will occupy us most, although it cannot be separated entirely from the others because most bodies of holy scripture contain accounts of a whole range of forms of a god's revealing either himself or his truths to his people. In the case of the Bible there are further difficulties because it is now known that many books are the work of several writers. This does not mean that God could not have been the author of it all in some sense, but it does raise a host of questions. The one, besides the authenticity of holy scriptures, which we shall focus upon is the question of the infallibility of holy scriptures. The question is why anyone should want to take them as infallible, as speaking the truth always, especially when our reason tells us the opposite. And we may well wonder just how much interpretation is possible before we give up trying to harmonize a biblical point with a rational one, or, more generally, why we should get involved in the obviously touchy business at all.

If one should cite the miracles associated with holy scriptures, this might only serve the skeptic's cause by pointing up the fact that we hear most about miracles in holy scriptures. So part of the credit given to miracles by a person in the twentieth century will come from the fact that they are reported in holy scriptures and part of the credit given to holy scriptures will come from the authenticity afforded them by the miracles and the prophecies associated with them. This makes for extremely complicated philosophical assessment of either. But, of course, a lot depends on whether we can make the notion of miracle plausible at all. In the post-Newtonian world, as we have seen, alleged miraculous phenomena are believed to be explainable scientifically or not to have happened at all.

Some of these points apply to the idea of immortality. In the twentieth century such an idea is extremely difficult to maintain, even for very religious people and even though there appears to be some empirical evidence, though very slim, that there may be psychic states continuing in some form for some time after a given individual's death. For many religious people the idea of immortality has to be accepted because it is sometimes suggested in holy scriptures and as genuinely miraculous. Here "miraculous" is used to suggest "contrary to all scientific understanding." Further, we shall see that some of the most interesting and appealing aspects of the doctrine of immortality have little or nothing to do with biological or psychological perpetuity and rather very much to do with their implications for the meaning of life as we know it now. I do not want to suggest that immortality in just this sense is not held as an article of faith based on holy scriptures. I shall, in fact, consider it as such as well. But I do want to suggest that we cannot merely examine the empirical possibility of immortality and have done with the doctrine when we are working in the context of philosophy of religion.

With these preliminary reflections in mind, then, let us take up each of the three topics in turn.

### Revelation.

The distinction between reason and revelation is not easy to clarify since the line between the two is subject to extensive debate among theologians. At one extreme some have claimed that revelation is something previously hidden from man disclosed to him from outside the normal sphere of knowledge and so something he cannot obtain but must have given to him. At the other extreme some have claimed that revelation is only one of several ways divine truths are known. From these two views and a whole range of middle views, the problem emerges of reconciling the truths of revelation with those of reason.

It seems to be implied in the first view that, his own abilities being limited, man cannot judge but must accept what is revealed to him. Equally, it seems to be implied in the second view that the truths of reason and the truths of revelation should be perfectly harmonizable. The former makes revelation the dominant form of knowledge so that we must insist on the claims found in holy writ no matter what our experience may tell us. The latter makes reason the touchstone of truth so that revelation becomes that which we must reconcile with reason. And all of this forces the question, What is special about religious belief that nonbelievers do not enjoy?

Specifically in this section I want to focus on the philosophical aspects of the notion of revelation. I can do this most easily by reference to two important philosophers who saw the possibility of conflicts arising between claims drawn from reason and claims drawn from revelation. It is particularly noteworthy at the outset that, though each philosopher sets out to offer assurance that conflicts will not, or at least need not, arise, each does it in a way not likely to be acceptable to the other.

St. Thomas Aquinas begins his attempt at harmonization by distinguishing between the two ways we know divine truths. First, divine truths may be known through reason, i.e. man's own natural sources of knowledge. Second, divine truths may be known through revelation, i.e. truths related by God for which man does not have to employ his reason to obtain. And some of these latter truths man could not have discovered through his reason had he tried. But this is the case only with some of these revealed truths.

For St. Thomas, then, the class of divine truths gained through reason and the class of divine truths gained through revelation overlap but they do not coincide. This means that some truths are both revealed and discoverable through reason, some truths are not discoverable through reason and so have to be revealed, and some divine truths are not revealed in scripture but discoverable through reason.

St. Thomas is concerned to hold that whatever knowledge is required for salvation has been revealed. Some people may find this redundant, but, he explains, God did not leave it to men to discover their need for and manner of salvation through their own resources. Some men do not have the ability to discover this for themselves, and many men do not have the leisure to discover this through philosophical pursuits.

It also follows on St. Thomas' view that men will have to receive some divine truths which their reason is not able to investigate. While there might be reasons for rejecting this consequence, St. Thomas argues that it is neither unfitting nor unreasonable. For, if it is the case that man is ordained by God for a higher good than man can tell in the present life, as Christianity specifically promises, then the only way he can be expected to strive for it now is by having this good made known to him through extrarational means.

Besides, St. Thomas adds, revelation makes us aware that God is above what we can think, thus strengthening our understanding of God and eliminating our error of presumption that the sole measure of truth is what appears to us to be the case. According to Aristotle, knowledge of higher substances is most loved by men even though they have little of it and it is this knowledge which brings the greatest perfection to the soul. Think, then, how much is added to it by revelation.[2]

St. Thomas further asserts that it is not foolish to give assent to the truths of faith. For, even though reason does not offer experimental evidence for them, assenting to them is not like believing in fables. "For these secrets of divine Wisdom the divine Wisdom itself, which knows all things to the full, has deigned to reveal to men." In revelation we experience the divine presence and grasp its teaching and inspiration. Now, rather than evidence appropriate to natural truths, revelation presents us with grounds appropriate to truths that exceed natural knowledge in the form of visible manifestations to works "that surpass the ability of all nature."[3]

These grounds are what we could put under the general heading of the miraculous. There are the spectacular cures of illnesses, the raising of the dead, the changes in the courses of the planets and stars, the inspiration given to human minds when they are filled with the gift of the Holy Spirit so that even simple, uneducated persons possess in an instant the highest wisdom and the readiest eloquence. These grounds, not other forms of persuasion such as the threat of force or the promise of pleasure, have led vast numbers of people, both simple and learned, to the Christian faith. Indeed, pleasures of the flesh are clearly spurned by these teachings.

For mortal men to accept these things is itself the greatest of miracles, but it attests to the authenticity of scriptures. So, too, must the rejection of visible and the love of invisible things be the result of divine inspiration. But all of this has not happened by chance. It has come from God as is evidenced from the foretelling of it by the Hebrew prophets.

Now, St. Thomas continues, contrast these grounds for accepting Christian scriptures with the grounds offered for accepting other scriptures and you will see whether or not it is foolish to accept the truths he claims are revealed by God. We must remember that St. Thomas' mission in this work is to demonstrate the truth of the Catholic faith, but he is, interestingly enough, involved in doing more than this. He is involved in showing that his faith is consonant with reason in a way that the faith of others is not.

Aquinas summarizes the case of Mohammed: Mohammed has seduced the people by promising carnal pleasure, thus appealing to human weakness. And to prove the truth of his doctrine he offers only arguments within the grasp of small intellects. He produced nothing miraculous, which is the only adequate sign of divine inspiration. Rather, Mohammed said he was sent because of his armed strength. This is a sign associated with robbers and tyrants. And among his first followers were men ignorant of all divine teaching. Through the strength of numbers, Mohammed forced others to follow him. Moreover, there is no witness borne him by the prophets whose testimonies he has forbidden to his followers.

The grounds, then, Aquinas offers for the acceptance of the Christian scriptures are the miracles, the prophetic pronouncements fulfilled, and their immense appeal to many men despite great governmental pressure to shun them. These do not fit scripture into the fabric of our natural reasoning about the world, but they do constitute reasons for believing in scriptures and they contrast admirably with many other kinds of grounds which might have been offered for them. They are good as opposed to bad reasons for believing—very good, in fact.

Now, given that men do have certain knowledge through their reason and given that we have divine knowledge through revelation, it follows, according to St. Thomas, that the two cannot conflict. Both are true and both come from God—the one through principles implanted in us by God and the other from God directly. Both form a unity in the divine Wisdom. St. Thomas offers further support for this view which we shall not consider. But his conclusion is clear and this is what interests us: "Whatever arguments are brought forward against the doctrines of faith are conclusions incorrectly derived from the first and self-evident principles imbedded in nature." [4]

Our reason, St. Thomas would say, builds its knowledge from experience of sensible things and these, being creations of God, retain a faint likeness to God. Thus reason can gain some knowledge of the truth of faith in the form of likenesses of it, but it can never grasp it so completely as to be able to comprehend it, i.e., reason cannot demonstrate on its own terms the truth of faith. One can in this life make progress toward the comprehension of divine truth by the use of his reason, but he can never penetrate the mystery fully. And, to insure man's seeking his salvation, God has revealed to man the requisite knowledge for salvation.

By the time we reach the seventeenth century, a distinct change in attitude has occurred. John Locke will present the distinction between reason and revelation in such a way that no claims said to be gained through revelation will be admitted to contradict any claim gained through reason. This is not on the face of it inconsistent with the view of Aquinas, but, as we shall see, the role of primacy with regard to truth has been reversed and it is now revelation which must make an account of itself before reason. It is not a matter of our reason's being limited in the face of revelation; or of its claims', which appear to contradict holy writ, resting on a probabilistic foundation only. It is now a matter of our not being able to assent to that which is clearly against our understanding.

In his major work, *An Essay Concerning Human Understanding,* Locke wants to draw a distinction between reason and revelation. He thinks lack of clarity here has fostered, if not disorder, many disputes and mistakes; and until clarity is achieved, disputes in matters of religion remain pointless. Every sect gladly uses reason as far as it can and where reason fails the issue is said to be a matter of faith and above reason. Now when we consider that anyone else can make this same move, even against others who make it too, it is obvious, he thinks, that nothing can really be settled.

Reason, as distinguished from faith, for Locke, is the discovery of truth or probability of propositions deduced from experience. Faith is the assent to any proposition not from reason but from trust in its source such as from God and through some extraordinary way of communication. This source of truths Locke calls revelation. So we are necessarily involved in faith when we discuss revelation in Locke's terms.

First, according to Locke's view of knowledge, more specifically the foundation of knowledge, nothing revealed directly to one man can by that man be revealed directly to another. Locke is prepared to admit that there may be special forms of experience whereby God supplies individuals with ideas; but, unless those with whom that enlightened individual wishes to speak have had those same ideas themselves, nothing he can say will impart those revealed ideas to them. So whatever was revealed to St. Paul, no matter what ideas, all he can say to others is that there are such things "as eye hath not seen, nor ear heard, nor hath it entered into the heart of man to conceive." [5] He is like a man who has a sixth sense trying to convey the content of experience through it to others who do not have it.

Second, the same truth may be contained in revelation which is discoverable by reason. Such a truth is of little use, though, if we can arrive at it by our natural means because we shall always be more certain of what we know for ourselves than of the proposition *that revelation came at first from God*. Think of the difference between assenting to the proposition that the three inner angles of a triangle equal two right angles on the basis of its being contained in scriptures, which one might want to do, and assenting on the basis of one's having demonstrated the proposition for himself. The same, Locke adds, holds for matters of sense experience. The story of the flood comes to us through revealed writing, but no one would say he is as certain of the flood as Noah, who saw and lived through it, or as one would be had he seen it for himself. All he has to go on is that it is written in a book supposedly written by Moses inspired. Nor is this so good as having seen Moses write it.

Thus the only thing which could possibly be of greater

assurance than our natural means of knowledge is direct revelation to us by God. But, even here, assurance can be no greater than our knowledge because we still have to settle in our own way that what we have received is indeed a revelation from God. But here, too, no alleged revelation can outweigh plain knowledge, or make a man rationally admit as true what is in direct contradiction to his understanding. We can never be as certain that something is a revelation as we can be that our reason tells us its contradictory is true.

Locke gives a helpful example: We are so certain that no body can occupy two different places at the same time that we could not rationally assent to any proposition which stated or entailed that a body was in two different places at the same time, no matter how many reasons were offered to support its being a divine revelation. For the evidence that we are not wrong in ascribing this proposition to God and the evidence that we have really understood the proposition can never outweigh the evidence of our own rational assent to the proposition that no body can occupy two different places at the same time. To maintain the opposite of this view would be to undermine the entire foundation of knowledge, destroying all difference between truth and falsehood while gaining nothing.

As Locke sums up, ". . . where the proposition supposed revealed contradicts our knowledge or reason, [it] will always have this objection hanging to it, viz. that we cannot tell how to conceive that to come from God, the bountiful Author of our being, which, if received for true, must overturn all the principles and foundations of knowledge he has given us." [6] Where one is considering assent to revelations conveyed to him by others as in the tradition of holy scriptures, he has to rely on reason even more than in cases of testing the truth of direct revelations to him. For he has to establish their authority. Locke is here directing his remarks against those who say they accept certain supposed divine truths on the basis of faith.

Third, Locke continues, there are many things about which we can have only very imperfect knowledge and others about which we can have no knowledge at all. These things are all beyond our natural faculties and so above reason. They are, when revealed, the proper matters of faith. That some of the angels rebelled against God and thus fell from grace, that the dead shall rise and live again, and other propositions of this sort are propositions with which reason has no direct relation. At best we can conjecture with only the smallest degree of probability, but we can never be certain. In these matters we should accept the revelation as truth, even if it goes against our conjectures, provided, of course, we are satisfied that the revelation is authentic.

This is the extent of the province of faith. So understood, faith does no violence to reason. There can be no doubt that what God has revealed is true, but whether in any given case we have a divine revelation or not is a matter for reason to decide. And no evidence can be adduced for revelation so strong that we will accept the revelation when it goes contrary to our reason. That is why it will not do to say we should accept something as a matter of faith even against our reason. We should allow divine revelation to supervene in matters of mere opinion or prejudice, but this does not violate the proper province of reason. Locke sums up his view by saying, " 'Credo, quia impossibile est,' 'I believe, because it is impossible,' might in a good man pass for a sally of zeal; but would prove a very ill rule for men to choose their opinions or religion by." [7]

We shall consider this last point further when we take up faith as such in the next chapter. Now let us notice the contrast between the views of Aquinas and Locke. Where Aquinas will say, "Whatever arguments are brought forward against the doctrines of faith are conclusions incorrectly derived from the first and self-evident principles imbedded in nature," [8] Locke will say, "There can be no evidence that any traditional revelation is of divine original, in the words we receive it, and in the sense we understand it, so clear and so certain as that of the principles of reason: and therefore nothing that is contrary to, and inconsistent with, the clear and self-evident dictates of reason, has a right to be urged or assented to as a matter of faith. . . ." [9] It is true that Aquinas and Locke are in agreement on the infallibility of divine revelation. For Locke, Scripture is infallible because if it conflicts with what we think is true, it must be either not of divine origin or we are not interpreting it properly. For Aquinas, Scripture is infallible because if a theory contained in it can be shown to be false by solid reasons, it cannot be held to be the *sense* of scriptures.[10] But there is an important difference in emphasis. For Aquinas the point is to demonstrate the infallibility of scripture. For Locke the point is to demonstrate the inadequacy of appeals to revelation against and in the face of reason.

We can gather from this comparison how important it is to become as clear as we can about the nature of appeals to authority, claims of infallibility, and the role of exegesis.

The third view we shall consider individually is that of the neo-orthodox theologian, Emil Brunner. It differs from the two we have just discussed in that it casts revelation in such a way that the tests of reason, man's natural basis of knowledge, are supposed to be made irrelevant to it. It is based on the idea that the living and personal God can be known only in personal encounter. This encounter is in God's personal word found in the Bible and only in the Bible. This idea is not unlike one of the grounds Aquinas offers to support his view that it is not unreasonable to accept Holy Scripture even though it goes beyond reasoned proof. But there is an important difference in that Brunner is not offering the personal encounter with God as a reason for assenting.

Revelation supplants reason and so is not bound by it. Brunner gives two reasons why this is so. Christian faith, especially as conceived in Protestant theology, is fundamentally different from every philosophy, all of which assume the ultimate validity of natural reason. Christian faith views the fabric of reason as having been pierced by revelation and it is upon revelation that the claims of theology are founded. In short, Christian faith recognizes a final authority different from that of philosophy.

Theology is the systematic or "scientific" expression of the Christian faith. It can lay claim to the title "scientific" only if it makes clear that its framework of grounds and consequences recognizes an authority different from other sciences. It must first make clear that all its claims follow from its own system of thought and only second must it put revealed faith and rational knowledge side by side for comparison. In this way Christian theology will not fall into the trap of making an account of itself before philosophy. What we have in theology based on revelation and philosophy based on reason are two separate systems each accounting in its own way for how all things hang together. We may note, finally, that for Brunner natural theology drops from the picture altogether.

Brunner's fundamental underlying notion is that Christian faith would cease to be faith if it sought to ground its affirmation on universal or rational truth. Revelation must supply its own ground or not be revelation; for only in it lies the personal encounter between God and man. Only in it can that which is otherwise hidden from man be revealed. For revelation is a supernatural kind of knowledge issuing from a region totally transcending the forms of man's natural knowledge. It is not propositional but personal knowledge and one does not gain it by scientific observation. Rather, he receives it as we receive knowledge of other persons, i.e., from the disclosure others choose to make of themselves and which we could not know had that choice not been made.

As I said at the beginning, this idea of personal encounter with God met in Holy Scriptures is the basis of

Brunner's view of revelation. Now it may help to make clear some of the preceding exposition if we examine further the nature of this encounter. It is certain that it will not come to much if it does not in some way take a realistic view of the Bible as a very complicated body of writing, with no one obvious God-man relation.

Brunner does not deny this. In fact he says

> above all, there is a variety of facts and processes that have the significance of revelation. God reveals Himself through theophanies, through angels, through dreams, through oracles (such as Urim and Thummim), through visions and locutions, through wonderful guidance given to human beings, and through the words and deeds of the Prophets. Above all the New Testament understands the person, the life, the sufferings, death, and resurrection of Jesus Christ, the Son of God, as the final self-manifestation of God, but again, not only Himself in His historical form, but also the witness given to Him by the Holy Spirit in the hearts of believers, the proclamation of Christ by His chosen Apostles, and through the believing community, and finally the fixing of this witness in written form in the Bible of the Old and New Testaments. Holy Scripture therefore does not only speak of the revelation; it is itself the revelation.[11]

Yet this does not mean that there cannot be "the" view of revelation in the Bible. The varied forms of revelation constitute a connected whole when we take them together from the right point of view.

To grasp this we must contrast the orthodox view of Scripture with Brunner's, keeping in mind as examples of the orthodox view those of Aquinas and Locke. On the latter view the Bible is a book of divinely revealed truth, a revealed thing or object. On what for Brunner is in "the unperverted view of Christian faith," Scripture is revelation only when "conjoined with God's spirit in the present." [12] Faith is contact with the absolute, hidden God, who reveals Himself to us personally as real in something real, namely Scripture in a measure as it is witness to the revelation of God in Jesus Christ. Now just as it takes telling in many ways to make a meaning clear, it takes many forms of experience to get across this single meaning of Scripture. To convey to us the meaning of Jesus Christ, we need the Old Testament, the New Testament, the epistles, and the gospels. Faith gives us the knowledge that this unity runs through all Scripture.[13]

We must be careful to avoid thinking that this is merely an *a priori* formula for separating revelation from what is not revelation in Scripture. This would make for the unity of an idea, but that is not what Brunner is trying to show. For him the point is not so much about what God revealed as that God revealed it. And this fact makes all the difference between something in Scripture being a moral commonplace or a heartfelt wish of a hopeful fancy and an authoritative communication and revelation of mystery.[14] Thus, Brunner adds, a word grasped in this way is different from a similar word in Lao-tse or Plato just because it is found in the Bible in actual conversation with God. Here we may note an important difference between what Brunner says is the attitude of Christianity to its scriptures and the generally recognized attitude of Buddhism to its.

This view supports well a view of exegesis which allows considerably more freedom from what on other views have proven to be embarrassing contradictions and unevenness in the writing found in Holy Scriptures. It is well known that the Bible contains contradictory remarks on the life of Jesus, legends have been incorporated into it, and there is a range in it from very faulty language to the highest quality literature. On Brunner's view the distinction between the human and the divine sides of Scripture becomes important, not as a way of avoiding the puzzles generated out of this complicated body of material, but as the very strength of the Christian faith.

Because Christians, on his view, do not have to take Scripture as a body of truths but as a source of contact with God, they may avoid bibliolatry. Christianity does not regard the Bible as an object of veneration, a book of magic, a fetish, even though the Bible is sometimes so misused. The Bible is not a book of oracles or a divine encyclopedia of infallible instruction on all subjects. Rather it is the word of God in a literary document which requires ongoing interpretation. And in this process revelation will occur from time to time to those who respond with faith.

This is a summary of Brunner's obviously very different view of revelation. We shall want to examine it along with the other two to see if any of them succeeds in making out a case for taking Holy Scriptures seriously. In doing this it will be helpful to go over some of the central concepts in a general context. Because this review will be done in terms of philosophical distinctions, we shall have to be especially careful in offering a critique of Brunner's view.

It is clear that all three of the views of revelation regard Holy Scriptures as an authority to which we may appeal for truth. There is nothing inherently unreasonable in appeal to authority, and we make it frequently in our lives in all kinds of situations. Much of a person's knowledge is based on authority and it alone. For example, I believe that cats require food, although I myself have never tested to see whether a cat might survive without it. I believe that arsenic will poison a cat if put in that cat's food, although I have never tried doing this. I would not even know what arsenic was without a label placed there by a pharmacist I trust. I believe that the moon is about 240,000 miles away from and orbits the earth. I have never measured this distance or traced the orbit with my own eyes. And I could continue with examples of this kind.

All of these in one way or another, and some in very complicated ways, involve an appeal to authority. The general formula for this reasonable process is shown in this question and this answer: "What reason do you have for sup-

posing *p*?" "I was told so by X." X may have depended on
the fundamental principles of science, and yet *my* appeal
to X would have been an appeal to authority.

But now from what has been said in connection with the
three views, it should be clear that an appeal to holy scriptures is no ordinary appeal to authority. On the contrary,
it is an appeal to an extraordinary authority. With the
clear exception of Buddhist scriptures, most sacred scriptures
and especially the Christian and the Moslem have been traditionally held to be the writings of men directly inspired
by God. The Koran is supposed to be a copy Mohammed
made of the very words of Allah. Aquinas wrote that "The
author of Holy Scripture is God," even though elsewhere
he speaks of Holy Scripture as "inspired by God." [15] If it
is reasonable to accept the word of the author of a book
about cats on the nourishment of cats, is it not even more
reasonable to accept the word of God as truth? Certainly
Aquinas and Locke are agreed on answering this question
affirmatively, at least as it stands here.

Any ordinary appeal to authority can, in principle, be
eliminated. I can allow my cat to go without food, or I can
put poison in her food, or I can try logging the moon's
course and even measure its distance from the earth, even
though it would be very difficult for me to do this myself
and may even require a space flight by me. Difficult or not,
I could in principle eliminate or, at least, know how to
go about reducing my dependence on authority. But I do
not. And this is not just because to do so is impractical,
but because it would be absurd for me to do so. I have
not the least doubt or reason to doubt the veracity of
these matters which I accept on authority.

By contrast, we may ask if all of this goes for Holy
Scripture. Is the authority appealed to here eliminable? Is
there reason to doubt the authority of Holy Scripture? The
first question dramatizes what we are dealing with when we
examine the appeal to the authority of Holy Scripture.
What would it mean to eliminate authority in this case?

Would it be to see for ourselves whether what is said in the Scriptures is true? For Brunner this is clearly impossible. And it is impossible, not just because it lies beyond our intellectual grasp as Aquinas might put it, but because the truth revealed in Holy Scriptures is wholly different from any truth we are capable of ascertaining for ourselves. Indeed for Brunner this truth in Holy Scriptures is completely self-authenticating. To grasp what is meant is to know it is true. Thus we are not really turning to Holy Scriptures as authority but as a source of experience or revelation to each of us. Unfortunately, he does not make sufficiently clear how there can be self-authenticating knowledge, a point which Locke would certainly raise. Nor does he make clear why it is to this particular set of scriptures that one ought to turn, why they are the authentic source of revelation.

Now to try to answer whether there is reason to doubt the authority of Scripture, we must do two preliminary things. First, we must pick a body of scriptures. This will, for the sake of the author's convenience, be the Bible. Second, we must remind ourselves that the only way we can properly begin to speak of truth or falsity or even doubt is to assume we are capable of settling upon what is said or what the alleged truth in question is. This, though obviously necessary, will prove difficult.

To close down some of the many variables in our problem, let us ask ourselves how we are to understand the claim "Scripture is an infallible authority." The insertion of the world "infallible" is not too much to add here because all of our authors on revelation are agreed that if we have divine revelation, it must be truth. But, strictly speaking, our claim is not equivalent to "Scripture is the word of God." For Scripture may be claimed as the word of God and still be denied to be infallible. God may not have wanted to give man an infallible authority. (However, Aquinas and Locke both state explicitly that God does not lie.) Also, one may hold an authority infallible and yet not identify this authority with God, or a god, or even an angel. Thus, Locke is prepared to make our natural reason the ultimate authority in matters of truth where we have a conflict between reason and revelation, although he would find the word "infallible" awkward when applied to this authority.

Suppose we try to show that the Old Testament is not an infallible authority by the following argument:

1. If the Old Testament is an infallible authority, every statement made in the text is true.
2. According to the Old Testament, the earth is (implicitly) said to be less than 6,000 years old.
3. But it has been shown conclusively by physicists that the earth is at least two billion years old.
4. Therefore, the Old Testament is mistaken and, hence, not infallible.

We have seen in Aquinas and Locke this move which we shall suppose is made now: Since it is conclusively established that the earth is more than six thousand years old, such a claim cannot be attributed to Holy Scripture, i.e., if a theory can be shown to be false by solid reasons, it cannot be held to be the sense of Holy Scripture. Clearly, showing that the Old Testament is not an infallible authority is very difficult. On the Aquinas-Locke view it will be difficult to establish the truth or falsity of any statement or even to establish definitely what any statement in the Bible asserts.

This means that the statement "Scripture is an infallible authority" is, on the view we are considering, not at all the same as "Every statement in the Scriptures is true"; for we are not left with the sense that there is a fixed list of statements in Scripture but, rather, with the sense that everything said there is subject to interpretation and reinterpretation depending on what kinds of solid reasons can be adduced for or against what is said. And this, it should be plain, depends on what men learn through the use of reason in science and humanistic studies. This explains in part what Brunner meant when he said that the task of biblical interpretation is an ongoing activity.

Moreover, the statement that Scripture is an infallible authority is, even in the very general sense of it suggested above, not going to be universal and categorical in the way a statement like "Every swan is white" is. In addition to the problems of singling out and interpreting specific claims in Scripture, we have to deal with something else, more like the attitude of the proponent of the statement. In saying "Every swan is white" a person has to be prepared to admit this statement is false should someone point to a black swan. And it is possible that there might be one. This possibility does not seem to be implicit in the thought of those who make the infallibility-of-Scripture statement; or, if it is, it is very hard to see what they could mean in attributing any authority to Scripture at all. They seem to be saying "If something alleged to be in Scripture is false, then it cannot be contained in Scripture." And this is very much like saying "If something alleged to be a swan is black, then it cannot be a swan."

It might seem to follow, and quite obviously, that the infallibility statement and all views of Scripture needing it reduce to triviality and therefore emptiness. It might seem that the attempt to preserve Scripture as an authority has come down simply to defining Scripture as an authority and compounds the error by defining it as an infallible one besides. If this is so, then to say "Scripture is an infallible authority" says nothing more about Scripture than saying "All swans are white" says about swans when the matter has been reduced to definition. The question, then, is, Why bother making such a statement?

There could be some point to it in the case of swans, as a kind of classifying procedure, although mere color is usually unreliable in biological matters. But why do such a thing with Scripture? Indeed, is it not very misleading to say the least and, one might even suspect, either a confusion or, worse, intellectual dishonesty?

While all this might seem to follow readily, there are reasons why one might want to hold to the infallibility of Scripture. We can begin to appreciate these reasons if we compare the infallibility statement to another statement, "Every effect has a cause." And when we do, we see that in one very important respect the two statements are alike. The cause-and-effect statement cannot, any more than the infallibility statement, be verified or falsified in the same manner as normal empirical generalizations. Where no cause has been found, as in the case, say, of multiple sclerosis, one might argue in defense of the statement that we have not looked long enough. Or one might argue, as in the case of cancer, that no cause has been found because no one cause exists, that there are many causes of cancer because we now know that there are many kinds of cancer.

Viewed logically, this latter form of defense is a reinterpretation of the matter in question. According to our statement, there must be a cause. It may be either that there is no cause (in which case, a clear negative instance having appeared, our statement is false), or that we have not looked long enough for the cause. The fact is, however, that we have looked for the cause of cancer for a very long time, much longer than we have looked for the cause of any other disease. So, then, we decide to reinterpret our problem. The question is, Why do we not consider the possibility that there is no cause, i.e., that the statement "Every effect has a cause" is false?

The point of these considerations is to see if the infallibility statement is anything more than trivial. The foregoing remarks show only that there is a parallel between it and the cause-effect statement. To pursue the parallel more fully to points of dissimilarity would not help us much in our main interest. I think we have seen that the truth or falsity of the infallibility statement cannot be established in the way the truth or falsity of any normal empirical generalization can. But we have also seen that it is still not trivial, no more than the statement "Every effect has a cause." Now it will be worth trying to see as well as we can what, if any, value it has.

One possibility is to say that the infallibility statement is neither true nor false, and is profitably construed, roughly, as a principle to the effect that: One should accept all Scriptural statements as true, while interpreting all Scriptural statements so that none is known to be false. Generally, we do not speak of their value as a guide or rule in some activity or operation such as reasoning or conducting a war. Following this possibility, then, we should ask if there is any value in holding to the principle about Scripture as stated just now.

Of course, there is a very obvious objection. It looks like a move to stave off the question of the truth or falsity of the statement "Scripture is an infallible authority" just because there is no reason to believe it is true. This would come dangerously close to Freud's view of the basis for the authority of all religious claims. They merit belief first, because our primal ancestors already believed them; second, because we possess proofs, which have been handed down to us from this very period; and third, because it is forbidden to raise the question of their authenticity at all.[16] It is this third reason which Freud says rouses our strongest suspicions because its only motive could be that we know very well how shaky the grounds for accepting are. Indeed, the claim that Scripture is divine revelation is itself a matter of religious belief and hence cannot be used to serve as an authority toward which to appeal religious beliefs.[17]

From a philosophical point of view Freud's point of refusing direct questioning is important. There is some reason to believe that the statement "Scripture is an infallible authority" would, given its form, ordinarily be taken to be a statement appropriately judged as either true or false. Denying this, as the suggestion would have us do, is an attempt to restrict the uses of "true" and "false" to statements not having the peculiar logical character of the one about Scripture. Taken merely like that, Freud would be perfectly right, and making the distinction would be perfectly wrong.

But there is a good reason for making the distinction, even so. In this way we do not confuse statements of the type in question with empirical generalizations. Their being more like logical rules than like statements of fact is pointed up. Now, though, the question is, Does this distinction, even if it is legitimate, make the rulelike infallibility statement more rather than less difficult to accept? Does not its new status constitute a psychological block to our accepting Scriptural statements? It might seem so because it might seem easier to accept the infallibility statement if we could think that it is true than if we could think only that it is worthy as a principle.

This would not seem to be the case with the causality statement. Let us construe the statement "Every event has a cause" as a maxim roughly equivalent to "Look for causes, predictive laws, etc." Not let us compare this with the statement "Since it is true that every event has a cause, this event must have one." Or we might compare it with an alternative formulation, "Since it is reasonable to search for causes of events, it must be reasonable to search for the cause of this event." Were we to reflect on what it would mean to say the statement "Every event has a cause" is true, we would discover that there is little logical difference between the statement formulation and the principle formulation.

On the other hand, there is considerable psychological difference between the two formulations. This is plain from reflection on how much more likely a scientist would be to persevere in his research if he says to himself "It is a fact that every event has a cause" than if he says to himself "It is a good idea to carry on research following the principle that every event has a cause." Yet if the difference is only psychological, then to someone who has thought about the matter rationally even this psychological difference becomes diminished. Whether one asks "Is the statement true?" or "Is the principle of value?" the answer to both comes to roughly the same thing.

So now let us take up the appropriate question: "What reason is there to believe that the principle of scriptural infallibility is of value?" The answer Brunner has given us is that Scripture is the word of God, and he thinks so because he believes it on faith. Not only this, but without faith the proper kind of self-authenticating encounter through Scripture between God and man will not occur. And for Brunner this is the end of the matter. But have we now reached the limits of rational discussion?

It would seem not because we can, and as philosophers we must, ask "Is such faith misplaced?" This seems to be what lies behind the strategy used by both Aquinas and Locke. Notice here that we are not as philosophers arguing against the legitimacy of faith. It may well be that faith plays a central function in religion. Nor does this mean that as rational men we may allow any appeal to faith that anyone cares to make. I do not want to go into the point here; it will be dealt with at some length in the next chapter. Here I only want to mention it with regard to the status of holy scripture, and emphasize the connection between faith and revelation.

Suppose we try to answer whether faith in the infallibility of holy scripture is or is not misplaced by giving the text in question very detailed examination assessing the probable effects of using the principle of infallibility with regard to that particular text. We would then, in effect, be asking, Does accepting the principle lead to desirable consequences when applied to this text? Notice before we go on that we might have the beginnings here of a way to assess the merits of one religious text over others.

Should we do this, we would find it an enormously difficult task. Indeed, when we think of doing this with the

Old Testament and the New Testament, with the Koran, or with the voluminous Hindu scriptures, it would very likely prove impossible to provide anything like conclusive evidence one way or the other for any one of these bodies of writing. This does not undermine the usefulness of our analysis. We still can say that if we were to see that undesirable consequences did follow, we would have shown that it is unreasonable to believe that using the infallibility principle is of practical value. In addition, it may well turn out that some specific case of scriptural interpretation could appear which we would want to take in a decisive way. It could happen, that is, that an inescapable interpretation of a sacred text required its believers to accept unconditionally the commandment to slay all unbelievers.

There is an objection to this analysis which in most religious discussions is inescapable. It is that our analysis shows only that use of the infallibility principle in connection with a certain body of scripture does or does not lead to desirable consequences in this life, but it leaves untouched the question of desirability of its consequences for the next life. But, since we do not know what are desirable consequences for the next life, anyone asking us to accept the principle of scriptural infallibility now would be asking us to accept more than this, namely, the principle that the principle of scriptural infallibility is valuable. And if this "higher" principle is not to be subjected to the same questions of empirical truth or falsity as the "lower," then we still must ask what are the consequences of following this principle—that the application of the principle of scriptural infallibility is valuable. And so there is no escape from an appeal to consequences on the level of this life, if we are to do anything short of just blindly accepting the principles.

Moreover, it should by now be clear that it will not help to say that holy scripture is the word of God as a way of avoiding an appeal to consequences. After all, part of what is at stake in our analysis is whether or not holy scripture is the word of God. Without an appeal to blind faith, we would have to appeal to the value of taking holy scripture as a guide—a guide to desirable consequences of a kind we are capable of evaluating. This does not, as we shall see, reduce to a matter of deciding what humans in their finiteness happen to like or enjoy at the time the evaluation is being made. Showing that holy scripture guides us to desirable consequences is not enough by itself to show that it is the word of God either. Accepting John Stuart Mill's *Utilitarianism* might, for all I know, lead to at least some desirable consequences, but that does not entail that the book is the word of God, regardless of how Mill might have thought of it.

So all the test of leading to desirable consequences establishes for a body of scripture is that it has met a necessary condition of its being the word of God. This test does not establish that the body of scripture has met a sufficient condition for being the word of God. This is as far as we shall go in laying out the conditions for its being so, but this will prove to have been going very far.

One of the major resting places for the case of the infallibility of any given body of scripture, then, is the moral value of the life that body of scripture would prescribe if the scripture were taken as infallible. This brings the focus back to the problem of deciding what is in scripture, i.e. what is being prescribed. Unless we can decide what is of highest moral value, we cannot decide whether it is to be found in scripture or not. This would seem to take us in a circle: the only way we can decide what the scripture tells us is by having an independent means of deciding what is of highest moral value. And so the old question comes back to haunt us. Why bother with Holy Scripture in the first place?

*Prima facie* it looks as if we have encountered a severe criticism of the worth of taking Holy Scripture as infallible, at least, as I have tried to make out what doing so would be.

But I believe that a procedure such as the one I have outlined would still be of great value. Following it would force
us to find the very best we are capable of finding out about
living because we believe the highest truth about our existence is to be found in scripture. Whatever limitations
would lie there would be our own limitations in finding the
best. The merit of the procedure would be that in following it we are striving for the best, at least, looking for it.

And, as for the question, why bother with scriptures, the
answer is plain. Holy scripture is not exhausted by what
we can immediately recognize as of highest moral worth.
There are many other prescriptions, usually implied, of
long-range import. The love-ethic of Jesus has applications
from immediate situations such as love of one's enemy to a
vision of the future when man may live with no war at
all. Unless we have moral knowledge to the contrary, we
try to follow these as best we can and to the extent that
we understand them.

It is even possible to view the vague hints of man's growing moral sensitivity as his gradual understanding of scripture or his now being able to grasp what lay in scripture
all along. Of course, religious skeptics would view them
quite differently, as man's imputing his moral knowledge
into the meaning of scripture. This brings us back to what
has been our main task here, and that is the quest for signs
of the authority of scripture. Although it would be extremely difficult to settle this last issue, there can be little
doubt that many moral insights, perhaps most major insights, have come from religious leaders who have drawn
inspiration either indirectly or directly from sacred writings.

Probably the most moderate statement of the view I have
put forth here was made by Dean Inge[18] who, I am
sure, is not the only other person to take this view. He
said that the best way of looking upon Holy Scriptures is
as a source of moral and spiritual insight which is inex-
haustible and flexible to the exigencies of life. The real
skill is in keeping alert to their rich and variegated insights

and not becoming frozen into any one set of formulations which may have proven practical for a certain time.

The analysis I have put forth contains a risky implication not contained by Dean Inge's view, or, at least, not readily elicited from it; and I want to draw it now because, appropriate to our purposes, it shows forth the status of holy scripture as it is in most religions. It is that of absolute supremacy in the governance of the believers' lives. Just as God is ". . . that living Being who is at once the ultimate existence and supreme and all-inclusive good" as well as ". . . that which we can, and must, worship," holy scripture is the expression of the meaning that Being has for our lives and so it too has a place of supremacy in matters of our conduct.

Finally, should holy scripture prove to be a framework too narrow, whose consequences for our lives are too limiting, the proper move for a rational man is, after due caution and modesty in making his assessments, to seek scriptures which can serve him. But, as we have already seen, such a clear-cut decision point is seldom, if ever, reached.

### *Miracles.*

It is particularly appropriate now to turn to the subject of miracles. Miracles are used to authenticate certain bodies of scripture, but in the contemporary view they may serve in just the opposite way, i.e., as stumbling blocks to those who may have found strong moral appeal in scriptural teachings but also strong revulsion to the counter-scientific thinking miracles imply. Miracles are often cited as proof of the unreasonableness of religious people, and they are most often derided by religious skeptics. Of course, our task is not to make apology for miracles, but to become as clear about them as we can be and then to pass philosophical judgment upon them. This means that we want to understand what they are or are supposed to be, whether there could in fact be any, whether any might have occurred and with what significance. So our work will be less a cataloguing than a logical exploration of some typical cases.

The function of miracle in religion is complex, and various aspects of miracle have been emphasized and de-emphasized by different people of different places at different times. Later in this section, I shall give a brief account of the variety involved. First, let me try to give some general idea of our subject. We begin with the definition suggested by the etymology of the word: "miracle is that which causes wonder and astonishment, being extraordinary in itself and inexplicable by normal standards; or as a sign indicating something other than itself." [19] Thus, not every marvelous phenomenon is religious. It must reveal or stand for something specifically religious.

Scholars usually exclude from the class of miracles the mythological accounts of the origins of the gods and their activities in the primeval past. They exclude as well the "inner experiences" such as visions, voices, and the like. This restricts the term to something like its ordinary sense, covering cases of divine intervention into the course of events or divine manifestation, as with impressive redirections of natural forces. Man both acts and is acted upon in certain miracles, as in cases of a man's being healed or even one man's healing another. Such events are very closely associated with most founders of religions as well as with holy men, holy places, and holy objects.

Part of the theological importance of miracles has already emerged in our discussion of revelation—the winning of assent to the truths alleged to be above reason in Holy Scripture. In this role miracles serve as a resting place for the case of the authority of Holy Scriptures. This is precisely one of the ways Aquinas saw them. But, within the religious experience itself, miracles occur as a way of establishing certain people as leaders or as prophets. For example, God tells Moses to lead the people of Israel out of Egyptian bondage, and this passages follows:

"But behold, they will not believe me or listen to my voice, for they will say, 'The Lord did not appear to you.' " The Lord said to him, "What is that in your hand?" He said, "A rod." And he said, "Cast it on the ground." So he cast it on the ground, and it became a serpent; and Moses fled from it. But the Lord said to Moses, "Put out your hand, and take it by the tail"—so he put out his hand and caught it, and it became a rod in his hand—"that they may believe that the Lord, the God of their fathers, the God of Abraham, the God of Isaac, and the God of Jacob, has appeared to you." Again, the Lord said to him "Put your hand into your bosom." And he put his hand into his bosom; and when he took it out, behold, his hand was leprous, as white as snow. Then God said, "Put your hand back into your bosom." So he put his hand back into his bosom; and when he took it out, behold, it was restored like the rest of his flesh. "If they will not believe you," God said, "or heed the first sign, they may believe the latter sign. If they will not believe even these two signs or heed your voice, you shall take some water from the Nile and pour it upon the dry ground; and the water which you shall take from the Nile will become blood upon the dry ground." [Exodus 4:1–9]

This passage illustrates that the people of Israel were not just waiting to believe any wonder they might see. It could take a great deal of miraculous performance to convince them. The assumption in the passage, however, is that they are prepared to accept signs should they appear authentic.

Another example is in this succinct passage, found in Deuteronomy:

And if you say in your heart, "How shall we know the word which the Lord has not spoken?"—when a prophet speaks in the name of the Lord, if the word does not come to pass or come true, that is a word which the Lord has not spoken; the prophet has spoken it presumptuously, you need not be afraid of him. [Deut. 18:21–22]

Finally, this example combines in the person of John the Baptist several features of the previous two examples:

The next day he [John the Baptist] saw Jesus coming toward him, and said, "Behold, the Lamb of God, who takes away the sin of the world! This is he of whom I said, 'After me comes a man who ranks before me, for he was before me.' I myself did not know him; but for this I came baptizing with water, that he might be revealed to Israel." And John bore witness, "I saw the Spirit descend as a dove from heaven, and it remained on him. I myself did not know him; but he who sent me to baptize with water said to me, "He on whom you see the Spirit descend and remain, this is he who baptizes with the Holy Spirit.' And I have seen and have borne witness that this is the Son of God." [John 1:29–34]

Other examples are to be found which demonstrate the power or even the status of a god, as when Elijah says:

"Answer me, O Lord, answer me, that this people may know that thou, O Lord, art God, and that thou hast turned their hearts back." Then the fire of the Lord fell, and consumed the burnt offering, and the wood, and the stones, and the dust, and licked up the water that was in the trench. And when all the people saw it, they fell on their faces; and they said, "The Lord, he is God; the Lord, he is God." [1 Kings 18:37–39]

But these and all of the other types might be related in a single way as illustrating the purposes of God. When we take them as so related, we can see the possibilities which exist for making the entire idea of miracle plausible. This point will become clearer as we proceed.

Tales of the miraculous occur throughout the world and it is very doubtful that the tradition of any religion is entirely free of them. In primitive and ancient cultures it is not easy to point out formal miracles, both because there is no well-articulated scientific conception of nature against which to contrast them and because certain kinds of divinely instigated activities just belonged to the accepted world order. Even without a scientific sense of causality, though, there are reports of extraordinary happenings serving in some of the typical ways miracles have served.

There may be a gradual de-emphasis on miracles in some religions as they mature. There is, for instance, more importance attached to more miracles in ancient Indian mythology than there is in the Upanishads and the Brahmanas, which regard the spiritual experience of religious insight as the only significant "miracle." This de-emphasis is not so clearly detectable on the level of popular religion.

There is also a difference in the amount of importance attached to miracles by the founders of a religion and their followers. It is said that Gautama Buddha had miraculous powers but he considered them devoid of spiritual significance. But within five centuries of the Buddha's death there appeared miraculous tales about the birth and life of the Buddha and later Buddhist saints, especially in the Mahayana tradition. In the introduction to the Jataka (i. 47), one of the five parts of the *Sutta Pitaka,* it is told how the future Buddha, awaiting birth, had become a superb white elephant, and from there he appeared to enter the womb of the properly purified queen who thus conceived without sexual intercourse; how the Brahmans announced this conception to the king telling him that he would have a son who would become a Buddha and savior of the world. And at the very moment of this conception the world suddenly shook and an immeasurable light spread through the sky. Then the scriptures go on, line after line, relating the wonders occurring throughout the world.

The New Testament tells of many miracles performed by Jesus Christ. I shall discuss one of them at some length presently. Many Christians believe that the miracles in the context of their faith have continued beyond the New Testament period, surrounding the lives and deaths of the Christian saints, and these stand among the requirements for canonization. Indeed, some Christians believe miracles are still happening, and among their outstanding claims are the reported occurrences at Lourdes.

The one major religious founder who rejected miracle totally was Mohammed. For him the Koran was the one and only miracle. But, the account of even his life has become surrounded with the miraculous as has all Muslim popular religion.[20]

It appears, then, that there are two distinctions to make about the role of miracles in each religion before we continue. The first is the difference between the religion as conceived by its founder and the subsequent investment of miracles by followers. The second is the difference between the presence of miracles in a religion, whether strictly associated with the founder or his followers, and the exact role of the miracles, i.e., whether or not they are essential to the religion. These distinctions make considerable difference to the credibility one might afford a given religion. Fortunately, this is more a job for religious apologists than for philosophers of religion as we understand the latters' task. But we cannot ignore these differences if we expect to make philosophical judgment.

Although much depends on the exact sense of "miracle" used, one might say that miracles are not essential to Buddhism in the way they are to Christianity. This is not to say Buddhism is free of what we today would call the supernatural. The idea of reincarnation, the idea of the Path, of Enlightenment, of Nirvana, and several others do not seem readily assimilable to empirical concepts. It is also believed that enlightenment will just lead to escape from the cycle of reincarnation; and this belief does not appear to be held in the same status as a falsifiable statement.

But reincarnation is not understood to be transmigration of the soul.[21] Indeed, it is not clear in Buddhist thought exactly what it is. And the Buddha did not say definitely whether the Enlightened ones exist after death, because he believed one could not speak of anything beyond existence.[22] So there does not appear to be any clear transcendent realm from which miracles could stem, even though the source, if any, of enlightenment is not explained.

When we add to these considerations Gautama's explicit repudiation of miracles found in the Kevaddha Sutta of the *Digha Nikaya,* the difference from Christianity becomes clear. Gautama is asked to perform a miracle to win converts, and he replies:

> But, Kevaddha, it is not thus that I am wont to give instruction to the brethren. Then that believer should announce the fact to an unbeliever, saying: "Wonderful, Sir, and marvelous is the mystic power and potency of that recluse. For verily I saw him indulging himself, in various ways, in mystic powers:—from being one he becomes multiform, from being multiform he becomes one: from being visible he becomes invisible: . . . he reaches, even in the body, up to the heaven of Brahma."
> Then that unbeliever should say to him: "Well, Sir! there is a certain charm called the Gandhara Charm. It is by the efficacy thereof that he performs all this."
> Now what think you, Kevaddha? Might not the unbeliever so say?
> Yes, Sir; he might.
> Well, Kevaddha! It is because I perceive danger in the practice of mystic wonders, that I loathe, and abhor, and am ashamed thereof.

For these wonders, the Buddha continues, compare very unfavorably with the wonder of education, i.e., the path to Arahatship. Such a response we may well expect from a religious leader or a man of great power, or a great teacher. It is even reminiscent of a lesson clearly present as Jesus is being tempted by Satan:

> And he took him to Jerusalem, and set him on the pinnacle of the temple, and said to him, "If you are the Son of God, throw yourself down from here; for it is written, 'He will give his angels charge of you, to guard you,' and 'On their hands they will bear you up, lest you strike your foot against a stone.' " And Jesus answered him "It is said, 'You shall not tempt the Lord your God.' " [Luke 4:9–12]

Again, we are reminded of the idea that in the Christian Scriptures miracles are not done without good reason. The truly religious does not need theatrics. As philosophers we might ask why this has come to be accepted. Is it because, as we may have suspected all along, there is no such power and we must seek reconciliation in something higher, or because the god's purposes really are above such use of power? In short, why should God and his appointed ones not use their power?

Yet an inescapable difference remains between Buddhist and Christian belief. There is one event which is clearly to be classed as a miracle which Christians make central to their belief, and that is the supposed resurrection of Jesus Christ. The same might be said about the incarnation of God in Jesus Christ, though to settle this point would require more discussion than space allows. The centrality of the resurrection is summed up clearly in these words of the Apostle Paul:

> If Christ has not been raised, your faith is futile and you are still in your sins. Then those also who have fallen asleep in Christ have perished. If in this life we who are in Christ have only hope, we are of all men most to be pitied. [I Corinthians 15:17–19]

This resurrection is also contained in the Christian creeds. It is so central that it would be extremely difficult to explain away while leaving the Christian faith intact, much as certain modern theologians might like to try.

We are, then, faced again directly with the task of assessing the reasonableness of believing that this event reported in Holy Scripture really occurred. We might get a better perspective on the problem if we compare two other accounts of resurrection from the dead, one in the New Testament and the other in the little known biography of Apollonius written by the second-century rhetorician Philostratus. The New Testament miracle is the raising of Lazarus from the dead by Jesus, and the miracle reported by Philostratus was performed by Appollonius of Tyana. Philostratus based his account on the report of one man, the memoirs of Damis, a disciple of Apollonius. The account of the raising of Lazarus of Bethany compares in this respect because it is reported only by John and not even mentioned by the Synoptists.

The account of the raising from the dead of a young girl by Apollonius goes as follows:

> Here too is a miracle which Apollonius worked: A girl had died just in the hour of her marriage, and the bridegroom was following her bier lamenting as was natural his marriage left unfulfilled, and the whole of Rome was mourning with him, for the maiden belonged to a consular family. Apollonius then witnessing their grief, said: "Put down the bier, for I will stay the tears that you are shedding for this maiden." And withal he asked what was her name. The crowd accordingly thought that he was about to deliver such an oration as is commonly delivered as much to grace the funeral as to stir up lamentation; but he did nothing of the kind, but merely touching her and whispering in secret some spell over her, at once woke up the maiden from her seeming death; and the girl spoke out loud, and returned to her father's house, just as Alcestis did when she was brought back to life by Hercules. And the relations of the maiden wanted to present him with the sum of 150,000 sesterces, but he said that he would freely present the money to the young lady by way of a dowry. Now whether he detected some spark of life in her, which those who were nursing her had not noticed— for it is said that although it was raining at the time, a va- pour went up from her face—or whether life was really extinct, and he restored it by the warmth of his touch, is a mysterious problem which neither I myself nor those who were present could decide.[23]

Philostratus is not highly trusted as an historian and his biography is considered to be somewhat fanciful. It is im- possible to ascertain the facts, and the memoirs of Damis are now regarded as probably a work of fiction. But the biography gained for Apollonius great religious veneration among the devout pagans of the later Roman empire. It did not, however, counteract the conversion effect which the reports of Christian miracles were having among the Romans, even though this may have been the motivation of Julia of Domna who asked Philostratus to write the life of Apollonius. But, to make our comparison more revealing, let us assume that Philostratus was among the trusted historians and the memoirs of Damis the testimony of a clearheaded, competent observer.

Did this resurrection really happen? Dozens of questions cross our minds. Even if the principal witnesses are not lying, which is not impossible, it may have been that they misinterpreted the situation. Could they have distinguished between a person dead and one in a deep coma? What criteria were used to determine death besides the cessation of certain bodily functions? Were life-suspending drugs known then and used? No one, I think, would let this evidence outweigh what he knows to be true about the finality of death, even though he has received most of the confirming evidence from the testimony of others. But the miracle of Apollonius, properly, should be taken as a possible negative case, since our claim about human mortality is basically an empirical generalization. Of course, there are also strong theoretical reasons, but these, at base, are empirical. Certainly, we would not, as a matter of course, say of a person we were convinced was not going to die that he was not a man.

In turning to the raising of Lazarus, we are struck by the context prepared for the miracle. At the beginning of John Chapter 11, Jesus receives the message from the sisters of Lazarus, Mary and Martha, "Lord, he whom you love is ill." Jesus responds, "This illness is not unto death; it is for the glory of God, so that the Son of God may be glorified by means of it." Next, it comes out that Jesus is going to Lazarus at great risk of his life because people are seeking to stone him in Judea.

Jesus' next remark directly about Lazarus is, "Our friend Lazarus has fallen asleep, but I go to awake him out of sleep." To this the disciples reply, "Lord, if he has fallen asleep, he will recover." The explanation then follows: "Now Jesus had spoken of his death, but they thought that he meant taking rest in sleep." Then Jesus says plainly, "Lazarus is dead; and for your sake I am glad that I was not there, so that you may believe. . . ."

Upon arriving Jesus finds that Lazarus has already died and has lain in the tomb four days. Martha comes to meet Jesus, while Mary sits in the house—some of those details frequently mentioned in biblical narration giving it a kind of intrinsic plausibility. Jesus says her brother will rise again, and she, thinking he means at the resurrection of the last day, concurs. Then Jesus says, "I am the resurrection and the life; he who believes in me, though he dies, yet shall he live, and whoever lives and believes in me shall never die. Do you believe this?" She replies, "Yes, Lord; I believe that you are the Christ, the Son of God, he who is coming into the world."

At the tomb Jesus commands the stone be taken away. Then the Scripture runs as follows:

> Martha, the sister of the dead man, said to him, "Lord, by this time there will be an odor, for he has been dead four days." Jesus said to her, "Did I not tell you that if you would believe you would see the glory of God?" So they took away the stone. And Jesus lifted up his eyes and said, "Father, I thank thee that thou has heard me. I knew that thou hearest me always, but I have said this on account of the people standing by, that they may believe that thou didst send me." When he had said this, he cried with a loud voice, "Lazarus, come out." The dead man came out, his hands and feet bound with bandages, and his face wrapped with a cloth. Jesus said to them, "Unbind him, and let him go." [John 11:39–44]

What Lazarus looked like after being four days dead is left to the imagination. The account does explicitly mention the state of deterioration of the body lest anyone suspect that Lazarus had been in a coma or under some kind of drug or post-hypnotic influence. But a point such as this, or any number of them, could not alone convince us of the truth of this resurrection any more than they could of the other. They serve to clarify exactly what is being claimed, that the witnesses had no doubt about what they saw, and that there were many people present, unbelievers as well as very ardent believers in the mission and identity claimed by Jesus.

We must note, also, that the account goes on to say that, after the event, a great deal of teaching and learning went on among the disciples and the converts. This and the context laid above help to make the contrast we are seeking. Both resurrections have about the same amount of historical evidence, but there is a context provided for the latter which does not exist for the former. This means that, even if we were to believe the miracle of Apollonius happened, it would be no more than a feat of magic, and this is almost to say to a modern man that it did not happen. Moreover, there seems to be no good reason to think anything of this kind should have taken place. It would at most amount to an impressive feat, make us marvel at the powers of Apollonius, and that is all. It is clear from the story in John that this is decidedly not what Jesus was doing. From the story in Luke we saw that Jesus had no interest in miracles for their own sake, for personal gain, or even for the mere gain of others.

The significant fact about the raising of Lazarus is that it is reported in Holy Scripture, which has a special authority because it is the record of events which happened in a community, reported by that community, and trusted by people today who are a continuation of that community. This is one main reason why Christians will contend that Scriptures have an authority greater than that of any other record. But the other, philosophically more important, reason is that there is a fittingness about the raising of Lazarus, and, it is contended by Christians, all other mighty works performed by Jesus which places them in a framework of rational purposes.

Specifically, the raising of Lazarus was to dramatize the mission of Jesus, and we have seen how the account is careful to record those things said which heighten this. This is the view taken by C. S. Lewis, who writes as follows:

> The fitness of the miracle lies in the fact that He who will raise all men at the general resurrection here does it small and close, and in an inferior—a merely anticipatory—fashion. For the mere restoration of Lazarus is as inferior in splendor to the *glorious* resurrection of the New Humanity as stone jars are to the green and growing vine or five little barley loaves to all the waving bronze and gold of a fat valley ripe for harvest.[24]

Here we have several themes converging in the dictum *Miracula sine doctrine nihil valent*—marvels without doctrine are worth nothing. Aquinas explains it as follows:

> Some things proposed to our belief are in themselves of faith, while others are of faith, not in themselves, but only in relation to others; even as in the sciences certain propositions are put forward on their own account, while others are put forward in order to manifest others. Now, since the chief object of faith consists in those things which we hope to see in heaven, according to Hebrews xi. I: Faith is in the substance of things to be hoped for, it follows that those things are in themselves of faith, which order us directly to eternal life. Such are the Trinity of Persons in Almighty God, the mystery of Christ's Incarnation, and the like; and these are distinct articles of faith. On the other hand, certain things in Holy Scripture are proposed to our belief, not chiefly on their own account, but for the manifestation of those mentioned above: e.g., that Abraham had two sons, that a dead man rose again at the touch of Eliseus' bones, and the like, which are related in Holy Scripture for the purpose of manifesting the divine majesty or the Incarnation of Christ; and such things should not form distinct articles.[25]

The credibility of miracles lies in their being reported in Holy Scripture, not just because they are reported there, but because they manifest some item of faith and thus fall into an intelligible framework whose meaning the faithful understand. It is true that part of the authority of Holy

Scripture is established in the minds of the faithful because of the miracles reported in them and thus possibly there is a circular argument at the base. But we must recall that not all of their authority comes from miracle and, moreover, not just any wonder counts as a miracle.

We can see more accurately what this means if we note that for the biblical writers a miracle was an extraordinary event but not something theoretically impossible, largely because there were no such theories. So for them the question of credibility was slight if it existed at all; for it was only natural to expect God to act in these ways. It was not until the biblically oriented church met with the many miracles in Greek culture that any such problem arose. And, even then, it was not a matter of doubting whether miracles occurred, but of sorting the authentic from the unauthentic ones. This was done along the lines I have suggested in the comparison of the two resurrection miracles.

For the Church Fathers, too, there would be no intrinsic difficulty in the idea of a miracle. For them the world order was not lawlike and it was itself in a sense as wonderful as the extraordinary occurrence, the miracle. Neither was less mysterious. And so it was that miracles were events standing beyond nature in its usual course, but not breaking the framework, certainly not standing against nature.

After the seventeenth century, and the development of the idea of a natural order governed by laws, the idea of miracles as exceptions to these laws which seemed to admit of no exceptions emerged. Christians felt that they must either give up the idea of miracles, at least as traditionally conceived, or find some way in which miracles were compatible with the scientific picture of the world. An obvious move was to suggest that God was the creator of this order (as even the natural theologians and most scientists of the time agreed) and so he could suspend his order when He willed. But, as more and more uniformities in nature were discovered, it became very apparent that he seldom or, perhaps, even never, for all we could tell empirically, so willed. Christians, both Roman Catholics and Protestants, had to lean on Holy Scripture for their evidence that the miracles did occur. This brought everything back to the credibility of the biblical witnesses to the miracles and, of course, the fittingness they found in the miracles.

This is the situation in which David Hume takes up the discussion in his *An Enquiry Concerning Human Understanding*, Sec. X, published in 1748. Hume takes as his point of departure Archbishop Tillotson's view of the foundation of Scripture. Hume states the view as follows: "It is acknowledged on all hands, says that learned prelate, that the authority, either of the scripture or of tradition, is founded merely in the testimony of the apostles, who were eyewitnesses to those miracles of our Savior, by which he proved his divine mission." [26] This means, says Hume, that for us now evidence for the truth of the Christian religion is already less than it would be had we had direct sensory evidence of our own. We are forced to rely on the testimony of others. And that testimony is for claims quite inconsistent with our own experience.

In matters of experience, there are all imaginable degrees of assurance as to the truth of a statement, from certainty to guessing. Being reasonable here means proportioning one's belief to the evidence, and where there is less than complete certainty that a statement is true there is a chance that the statement is false. One must weigh the evidence of one side against the other to decide which is more probable. Now in the case of using human testimony as evidence for our beliefs, we must remember that, important and useful as using it is, the statement "Human testimony may be trusted" is itself only a probability statement. Its probability is based on our experience. We generally trust people to tell the truth because they are motivated to do so, but there are people whom we do not trust for various reasons. And just how we count human testimony depends on exactly what is being claimed, how reliable the witnesses are, how many of them are there, whether they contradict one another, just how they act when they tell us, etc.

Even if all things would be favorable for accepting a given testimony, there are some statements we would not believe no matter who told us, and these are statements which contradict what we have through long experience come to expect. This is just the situation we are in when we are dealing with miracles. A miracle, Hume says, is a violation of the laws of nature.[27] There must be a uniform experience opposed to every miraculous event for it to deserve the name "miracle." But it is just this uniform experience which stands as full and direct proof against the existence of *any* miracle.

Moreover, no proof so full and direct can be destroyed, nor any miracle made credible, except by an opposite and superior proof. It follows readily in Hume's mind that the following maxim is worthy of our assent: "No testimony is sufficient to establish a miracle, unless the testimony be of such a kind, that its falsehood would be more miraculous than the fact which it endeavors to establish." And, even though the balance of evidence might thus be reversed, this alone makes the miracle only minimally likely.

But, whether or not it is logically possible that a reasonable argument for a miracle might be made out, there has never been in the history of mankind a miraculous event with anything like the required evidence. There has never been a miracle with enough qualified and properly motivated witnesses. People are fascinated with that which causes surprise and wonder as miracle does, and so they want to believe it happened and to become involved with it. All accounts of miracles and the supernatural abound among ignorant people. Such events never happen in our day among us. Different religions claim their own miracles as a way of authenticating themselves against each other and thereby destroy the credit of all miracle claims.

So when we combine Hume's maxim with the reasons

for holding to the fallibility of human testimony, we are forced to conclude that no testimony for any miracle has ever even amounted to the probability, let alone proof, of a miracle. Before going on we should ask ourselves on the basis of all we have considered in connection with miracle and revelation if, theoretically, there ever should be adequate proof, would the event in question cease to be a miracle and become a natural event?

C. S. Lewis objects to Hume's treatment of miracles. He sums up Hume's view as follows:

> Now the regularity of Nature's course, says Hume, is supported by something better than the majority vote, or, as Hume says, by "firm and unalterable experience." There is, in fact, "uniform experience" against Miracle; otherwise, says Hume, it would not be a Miracle. A miracle is therefore the most improbable of all events. It is always more probable that the witnesses were lying or mistaken than that a miracle occurred.[28]

To this Lewis objects that Hume has presupposed in his argument that miracles have never happened. To say there is absolutely uniform experience against miracles, is to say miracles have never happened. With this presupposed, then, of course miracles never have happened. But to know this we must know that all miracle reports are false, and to know this we must know that no miracles ever happened. This is begging the question.

Lewis further objects that Hume's idea of probability rests on the principle of the uniformity of nature—that what has happened with regularity will continue to happen. This principle cannot be proven by experience because past uniformity does not establish future uniformity, nor does experience even make it probable. Had Hume been consistent with himself, he would not have forgotten this.

Then Lewis goes on with this analysis:

The question "Do miracles occur?" and the question, "Is the course of Nature absolutely uniform?" are the same question asked in two ways. Hume, by sleight of hand, treats them as two different questions. He first answers, "Yes," to the question whether Nature is absolutely uniform: and then uses this "Yes" as a ground for answering "No," to the question, "Do miracles occur?" The single real question which he sets out to answer is never discussed at all. He gets the answer to one form of the question by assuming the answer to another form of the same question.[29]

Thus Hume finds no room for miracles within the natural framework.

But Hume did not set out to ask whether miracles ever occurred. He set out to see upon what basis we believe that they occurred. He has asked what a reasonable person would do and decided that he would not accept a miracle report for the usual reasons one accepts reports on other matters. This is one reason why Hume would see a difference between the two questions which Lewis identifies. For Hume the procedures we use to reason about matters of fact will not help us just because a miracle by its nature must constitute a break with matters of fact.

Of course, whether a miracle must go against the laws of nature to be a miracle depends on whether a singular event might be called a miracle. This would be an event which is, say, historically unique and having other characteristics of miracle, such as being a portent. And so Hume may be overdoing the point. Nevertheless, if he is at all serious in the conclusion to that section of the *Enquiry,* he has taken us to the heart of the matter. For he insists that the Christian religion is founded on faith, not reason, and to confuse the two is surely to make religion impossible. Unless there is some faith commitment, no one will be able to accept the Scriptures. Miracle stands against the laws of nature because it stands outside the framework of our normal network of explanation, not because it is logically impossible.

Thus the value of Lewis' criticism is not in showing that Hume has begged the question, nor even in showing that Hume's acceptance of the principle of the uniformity of nature is not empirically grounded. The value lies in his pressing the discussion to its ultimate point: the belief that the world is and always has been uniform is of the same status as the belief that miracles occur and, from our earlier consideration of the principle of causality, holding to either or both principles appears to be something very like what subsequent theologians and philosophers have called an act of faith.

Even if Lewis had pressed this point against Hume, this would not have been an embarrassment for Hume. Hume was among the first to insist that holding to the principle of causality is not itself rationally justified: it is presupposed in our reasoning, and so something he calls natural belief. Whether Hume was serious or not in his last remarks about the need for faith in accepting miracles, his treatment has shown the clear need to discuss the concept of faith and how much depends upon it. This will be the subject of the next chapter.

Before leaving the subject of miracles we should note that during the nineteenth century many theologians gave up the idea of miracle as dramatically counterscientific. They tried to hold that miracle so conceived was not essential to Christian belief. The theologian Friedrich Schleiermacher tried to square miracle and the rigidly ordered Newtonian world view by making miracle itself a natural event as viewed by a person of religious understanding. This view is hardly compatible with Christian belief as we have interpreted it so far, and as other theologians of Schleiermacher's time apparently thought too. They responded to the problem of miracle simply by de-emphasizing miracle and emphasizing the moral and religious transformation effected by a response to Holy Scriptures. This move, of course, is already to be found in Aquinas.

At present, the prospects for the miraculous seem brighter because of the less mechanistic scientific views being held. Again, the idea of faith becomes more important both for scientists as they become more aware of the nature of presuppositions of the sciences and for theologians as they become aware that there are such presuppositions. The shape of the discussion, we may expect, will be along the lines intimated by Lewis' objections to Hume.

Finally, while we shall see that much will depend on the concept of faith, the preceding discussion does not inevitably lead to the conclusion that all depends on faith. And, while the arguments of Christians and others for their belief in miracles on the basis of holy scriptures have not convinced us, I hope our examination of their belief and evidence make miracles less outrageous than they might have appeared at first.

### Immortality.

That a man once dead should live again or that a man should live forever strikes most men as nothing less than a miracle, and yet belief in human immortality is practically universal. This belief takes many forms and before we can pass judgment on it we shall have to consider some of its forms to see just what is meant by immortality. But not even then should the reader let this be his final judgment. There are, after all, several chapters relevant to immortality following in this introductory book, and immortality is a very large topic.

When one tries to get some of the claims about immortality clear, he meets right away with two difficulties. First, the word "immortality" covers many matters and has associated with it many more. Second, and more basic, the subject alleged to be free of death, temporary or permanent, in immortality claims may be one of any number of things, depending on a lot of other beliefs and influences in the mind of the person making the claim. To some it is the mind of the dead person which is said to continue living. To some it is the reintegrated, resurrected body of the dead person which is said to come to life again. For others it is the so-called soul of the person which is said to continue.

The only way I can take account of the first difficulty is to say here that I shall discuss only several aspects of the topic, those I judge to be most clearly related to the general purposes of this book. As for the second difficulty, I shall try to spell out the exact subject of each claim as I examine it. I believe it is safe to begin some general remarks using the term "life" to refer to all of the subjects of these immortality claims because, in general, "immortality" refers to a supposed life after death.

To move toward the subject, though somewhat indirectly, it may be all right to say that what continues after a man's death is his life. This would cover many primitive notions of immortality and also indicate the basis of thinking about immortality. It is that about a man which distinguishes him from a corpse that people are talking about when they talk about his spirit, soul, or even ghost. It includes many aspects of the person from his reason to his voice or even a kind of shadow of him as he is or was normally experienced. Just what is included depends on the notions and theories of the people whose view of immortality is being considered.

One relevant, specifically philosophical issue is the question of what keeps these aspects together. Just how this is settled has profound implications for the validity of any religious doctrine of immortality. It bears on whether the doctrine is at all intelligible, whether the immortality is the survival after death of a certain person and for how long. One kind of answer given is that the soul is itself a substance independent of matter. This view might be attributed to Plato, if we are not trying to be extremely accurate. For Plato the soul of each man is "immersed" in a body and thus becomes incarnate. At the time of death the soul of a man is released. His body decays, naturally, but his life continues. The soul continues because it is itself of eternal substance while the body is not. This means that the man living as we know him is both a mind and a body, and that the same man continues after death forever just because that is the way the soul is. This influenced a great tradition in philosophical and religious thought, having its major impact with St. Augustine and Descartes.

Aristotle held a different view, rejecting the idea of the soul's being able to stand independently of the body. For him the soul was the form of the body, something like the expression of the totality of what the body of a fully active man could do. Aristotle made an exception of the intellect which he thought could function independently of the body and so may continue after bodily death, but he did not develop the notion and so left it unclear whether one could, strictly speaking, say that a person survived death. Aristotle's view had its own influence on Arabian and Christian thinkers who developed it in different ways. For example, the Moslem philosopher Avicenna (980–1036) held the individual soul was eternal, but Averroës (1126–1198), also a Moslem, held only reason as such was, and Aquinas formed a Christian interpretation of immortality based on Aristotle.

The views of both Plato and Aristotle, to the extent the latter was committed at all to the immortality of individuals, because of the eternal nature of the substance entailed, are properly called unconditional immortality. No matter what a person does in his natural lifetime, he will continue in the stated form after his death. Plato believed that what a man does will have an effect on his afterlife which may or may not be agreeable to him, but each man will nevertheless survive death whether he likes it or not just by virtue of the nature of soul.

In two respects Plato's view compares to the Hindu and, with certain qualifications, the Buddhist views of immortality, according to which a man goes from one incarnation to another, and exactly what kind the next will be depends on what he does in the present one. By the Hindu and Buddhist law of karma one may, through excellence of conduct and attitude, find release from this cycle and gain eternal bliss. Exactly what that final bliss might be has not been made precise, even though there are some detectable variations among the different religions. Plato held that the soul became incarnate and strives for release, but it is difficult to determine how committed he was to the idea of a reincarnation cycle.

Since the Renaissance, an entirely different line of thought has been gaining ascendency, one which picks up the Aristotelian emphasis of the dependence of soul upon the physical body. That this should have happened is understandable in light of the rise of interest in the physical sciences and the frequent attempts made to understand all phenomena in terms of them. Following this line of thought, continuity of soul is rejected because the soul's fate is so intimately connected to that of the body. Apart from ideological considerations, it is clear that a great deal of what in the past has been attributed to soul can be accounted for in terms of physiological processes. Discoveries in the field of brain physiology and research into the influences of chemicals such as LSD upon the so-called inner, mental states support these reflections.

On this line of thinking it becomes extremely difficult to conceive of what it could possibly be that did survive death. The identity of the person is not to be found in the continuing existence of a single substance known as the soul, but is in a combination of factors such as the person's own memory and, that failing, his physical characteristics. And this leads to the further question, extremely difficult for those who hold to survival: What would it be for a person to survive death without his body whereby during his natural lifetime he performed certain acts and appeared to himself and others, especially when there is now reason to associate very closely the operation of memory with the physical organ, the brain? He would have no sense organs, no kinesthetic or any internal sensations of pleasure or pain, and probably no memory.

To these difficulties we must not forget to add the apparent continuity in form from animals to men and the doubts it raises. If men survive death, then why not animals? If either or both are destined for something after death, why are they now so subject to the workings of blind and tragic accidents?

All of these reflections seem to fit with a highly naturalistic view of man. Attempts to re-emphasize the spiritual in man, such as in the work of C. G. Jung, have little effect on this naturalistic view because it is so powerful in explaining and integrating psychological phenomena. When we add to this the effect the application of cybernetics to the understanding of human behavior by providing models of self-regulation, there seems little left of that divine spark in man.

C. J. Ducasse, one of the rare exponents of the belief in survival after death, has objected to this line of thought.[30] He objects, first, that the identity of thought or consciousness, the core of personality, has not been established. The words "thought," "feeling," "sensation," "desire," and the like do not name either chemical or behavioral events, as anyone of us can easily assure himself directly by introspection. There is not the slightest resemblance between these two kinds of entities, and to try to equate them is to toy with the meanings of words as one who would say "wood" is another name for glass. There is a connection between these two kinds of entities, but it is not one of identity.

He objects, second, that not even the strict dependence of the mental on the physical has been established. The behavior of people is affected by alterations of their physical condition, but this only means that the bodily signs of consciousness are affected, not consciousness itself. Think of when we are asleep and dreaming. Whether we remember our conscious processes does not affect the possibility that we had such consciousness, as reflection on our early childhood, which we cannot remember but during which we must have been conscious, readily shows.

He objects, third, to the idea that states of consciousness cannot continue without the body because of the causal influence of the body required to produce mental states. This, he says, is true only of some mental states, and there are other mental states which produced bodily states such as one's willing to raise his arm and doing so, thinking of eating and his mouth watering, or suffering psychological trauma and not being able to walk. The fact of interaction of mind and brain in cases such as these is compatible with the action of mind and brain independently of each other.

To the idea that consciousness evolved as the nervous system became more complex in animals and then man evolved, Ducasse objects, fourth, that the converse might also be said to have happened. Various mechanisms of the body may have been produced by cravings for them. And, finally, as to the haphazard way in which men are born and die, Ducasse points out that nothing at all pertaining to the question of survival follows logically from that fact.

Ducasse considers himself to have shown that all of the arguments against survival are very weak and show nothing about the likelihood of survival. This makes him wonder why there are people who find them convincing. The answer he finds is in their metaphysical bias—"*to be real is to be material,* and to be material . . . is to be some process or part of the perceptually public world." Now no matter how useful this assumption is in investigating the physical properties of material things, it will always limit one's horizon to physical causes and effects and preclude his consideration of nonmaterial ones.

If we reverse the process and think of our awareness first, we can think of the material world as just one among other objects of our consciousness known through the operation of the mind. This should shake us from the exclusive use of material explanations of all phenomena. The material world is not the source of explanation; the mind is.

There is another aspect of this discussion more or less restricted to the philosophical views of survival which we must mention before turning to the more specifically religious views. This is the matter of what, if anything, spiritualism and psychical research add to the considerations bearing on the question of survival. Stories of appearances and communications with the dead are found even among the ancients. In modern times attempts have been made to produce definite evidence of the existence of souls. Spiritualism attempts to relate in various ways to souls. There have been claims of success in mediumistic trances, automatic writing, and other alleged nonphysically caused physical events such as tapping and table-lifting, and even reincarnations.

Psychical research, the investigation of such reported phenomena, is an attempt to determine if these things really do happen. There has been no widespread acceptance of some of the positive results which have been reported. It seems likely though, that if such results were to be obtained, some of the laws of the physical sciences would be changed or, at least, require supplementation. Even so, the same problem noted in the Ducasse discussion would come back to haunt us. We would be seeing from the empirical side the difficulty raised conceptually about just what it would be with which we are in communication. For no mere tapping or table-lifting, no matter how well established as a psychical phenomenon, proves that the individual survives death. It may be that some part of the individual survives, but this part may be of small interest and comfort to one contemplating his death. It should even be frightening to consider what such an existence might be if we were to experience it, and if it makes sense to speak of experiencing it. This prospect weighed against suicide in Hamlet's mind, understandably.

With this conclusion about the prospects offered by psychical research and with the knowledge that Ducasse can at best show only the possibility of survival, it is no surprise that many thinkers have tried to show that there really is no need to be interested in survival after death. For them men can accept this life as quite enough because what men really desire is fullness of natural life, that satisfaction of impulses too often repressed, and enough time to get that satisfaction. To this has been added the thought that a life of retarded aging, even interminable natural life, a prospect not entirely ridiculous in our time, would be sheer tedium and, before many years, something from which we would all want desperately to be released.

Some of Santayana's reflections on Lucretius' view of death bear along these lines.

> There is, or there might be, an art of dying well, of dying painlessly, willingly, and in season—as in those noble partings which Attic gravestones depict—especially if we were allowed, as Lucretius would allow us, to choose our own time.
>
> But the radical fear of death, I venture to think, is something quite different. It is the love of life. . . . The love of life is not something rational, or founded on experience of life. It is something antecedent and spontaneous. It is that Venus Genetrix which covers the earth with its flora and fauna. It teaches every animal to seek its food and its mate, and to protect its offspring; as also to resist or fly from all injury to the body, and most of all from threatened death. It is the original impulse by which good is discriminated from evil, and hope from fear.
>
> Nothing could be more futile, therefore, than to marshal arguments against that fear of death which is merely another name for the energy of life, or the tendency to self-preservation. For what is most dreaded is not the agony of dying, nor yet the strange impossibility that when we do not exist we should suffer for not existing. What is dreaded is the defeat of a present will directed upon life and its various

undertakings. Such a present will cannot be argued away, but it may be weakened by contradictions arising within it, by the irony of experience, or by ascetic discipline. There would be the true means of mitigating the love of life; and if the love of life were extinguished, the fear of death, like smoke rising from that fire, would have vanished also.[31]

These reflections belong with those of people who believe it is possible for a man to make a natural adjustment to the fact of his death.

Unfortunately, it may not be possible for all men to accept death, even if some can. Nikos Kazantzakis has his life-loving hero, Zorba, and Zorba's boss say, of death:

". . . Some grow dizzy and delirious, others are afraid; they try to find an answer to strengthen their hearts, and they say: 'God!' Others again, from the edge of the leaf, look over the precipice calmly and bravely and say: 'I like it.'"

Zorba reflected for a long time. He was straining to understand.

"You know," he said at last, "I think of death every second. I look at it and I'm not frightened. But never, never, do I say I like it. No. I don't like it at all! I don't agree!"

He was silent, but soon broke out again.

"No, I'm not the sort to hold out my neck to Charon like a sheep and say: 'Cut my throat, Mr. Charon, please: I want to go straight to Paradise!'"

I listened to Zorba in perplexity. Who was the sage who tried to teach his disciples to do voluntarily what the law ordered should be done? To say "yes" to necessity and change the inevitable into something done of their own free will? This is perhaps the only human way to deliverance. It is a pitiable way, but there is no other.[32]

It is this same paradise-longing rejected by Zorba which the modern humanist rejects as detracting from the importance of this life.

This longing for immortality has itself been made the basis for the belief that we have it. Of course, our feeling or even our desire for immortality, no matter how strong, is hardly an argument for the immortality of the soul.

There is usually lurking in arguments of this kind a pre-supposition that there is a rational economy in the world as a part of God's plan, and that the desire for, or expectation of, immortality would not have been implanted in us unless we were to expect it. There must be a realm, so the thinking goes, where the tragedies and ironies of this life, especially the fact of death, are reconciled. This thinking comes very close to the specifically religious views we shall consider shortly.

Perhaps a more rationally defensible view is that taken by certain philosophers, usually of idealist tendencies. It takes account of the sense of the eternal possessed by man, but does not equate immortality with survival after death. Much depends on what view one takes of the nature of thought, and we shall not be able to examine this part of the idea. But I present one informal statement of the view by Benedetto Croce because it is a philosophical representation of the religious doctrine we shall consider next.

> The Life Eternal is not only to be vainly hoped for in a "beyond," but something we already possess and experience in every action, whenever we know a truth, realize beauty or do a good act. How else would we have come to the thought or name of "eternal life"? In every one of such acts we feel that we have put off our corruptible, mortal body, and raised ourselves with God. For that very reason it is absurd to desire or demand or conceive a life eternal for that part of ourselves which is only instrumental to those other parts in whose service it is worn away. Our bodily, "organic" life is by definition transient and perishable; it is precisely the not-eternal stepping-stone to something higher, constantly abandoned in our advance.[33]

This may be the most hope nonreligious thinking about the soul can give us—possibly survival after death but in an unknown manner, or possibly immortality but without survival after death.

It is true that these views have influenced and have been influenced by religious doctrines of death, survival, and immortality. But there are certain differences which make a separate treatment of the religious views necessary. I believe it is safe to say there are no religious doctrines of mere survival and the subject is of very little relevance to religious doctrines. At most it may be taken by believers as *prima facie* evidence for their doctrines.

Philosophical grounds might even be at odds within religious teaching. One obvious reason is the special conduct involved in immortality doctrines of the religions. We have seen that with Plato man is immortal and only his experiences in the afterlife will be affected by his conduct in this life. With the Hindu views the very life into which one is to be reborn is determined by his conduct in the present one. But in Christianity one's immortality is conditional upon his having earned it, according to some theologians, or his having been given it by God, according to others, or both, according to still others. In any Christian view, immortality is not a foregone conclusion.

It is true that the Buddhist scriptures deny the existence of the inner essence of the human personality, the *atman* of the *Upanishads*. The human self is a heap of elements, not an enduring substance. Meditation reveals the self to be illusory. Thus Buddhism's doctrine of self is not far different from that of the modern Western culmination of Aristotle's tradition. But Buddhism, as a religion, maintains that this insight must be gained as a necessary step in salvation—a liberation, perhaps, from one's own ego-terror.

The Christian doctrine of the afterlife is so different from views of the eternal soul-substance that it is properly called the doctrine of resurrection. For Christians the body is supposed to be resurrected. This makes it more intelligible in one respect: it mitigates the problem of visualizing what the existence after death might be and, more philosophically, sets aside the question of how a disembodied mind or spirit could exist. What is promised is that the whole person will live again in a new age. How his body will be made so that it will not wear out in the future remains a mystery. There are other well-known difficulties. If the reader is not aware of them, he will be as soon as he tries to think concretely about what would be required for this event to occur.

There is a view allegedly based on the Gospels which is relatively free of these difficulties.[34] It emphasizes that aspect of the Christian hope found in such expressions as "being born from above," "putting on Christ," and living "the new life." The Greek word for life in this sense is *zōē* and it contrasts with *bios* meaning life span, and with *psyche* meaning the animating principle. What man should find in the new life is not an unending span of life but a certain quality of life, marked by participation in the eternal much as Croce characterized it. Death is not something we shall survive, but we shall overcome it by following the way of life taught by Christ. This view is typical of recent attempts to reinterpret religious doctrines in terms of behavior in this world. This does not make it any less interesting, however.

To conclude this discussion, I want to return to the more orthodox view in order to relate the belief in immortality more closely to the other two topics of this chapter. Religions have perpetuated the doctrine of an afterlife, but not as a philosophical hypothesis, because the question of empirical evidence is practically irrelevant to it. And for Christians, it is something hoped for but not established empirically and not assured to anyone. The claim that individuals find assurance in their experience is often heard among religious writers, but the basis for the hope is in the Christian Scriptures. Theologians point to the biblical promise of a future life given by Jesus to the robber crucified with him and to the dramatization of a future life in the resurrection of Jesus Christ.

# III

## Faith

*Introduction.*

Faith is a fundamental notion in religious thought, and is for philosophy of religion the key concept. It occupies a central place in Christian thought. Its classical definition comes from the Epistle to the Hebrews: ". . . faith is the assurance of things hoped for, the conviction of things not seen." [1] This formulation attributed to Paul has had a major influence on subsequent Christian theology. Many variations of this definition have been offered, partly in response to extra-theological developments. As we shall see, certain modern definitions seem to go so far as to reverse this original one.

Faith is central because all authority, even reason, is said to depend upon it. In preceding chapters we have seen how the acceptance of holy scripture depended in part upon the acceptance of miracles, and how acceptance of these and the authority of human testimony depended upon whether we believed such things could have happened as reported. We have also seen how acceptance depends on our being disposed to credit certain testimony because it was part of a tradition of trust and fit in with our view of things in general.

Faith gives us the comprehensive grasp of reality needed for understanding. Behind faith lies the notion *credo ut intelligam,* I believe that I might understand, and it comes from Isaiah 7:9—*"Et caput Ephriam Samaria, et caput Samariae filius Romeliae. Si non credideritis, non permanebitis."* In English it reads: "And the head of Ephraim is Samaria, and the head of Samaria is the son of Remaliah. If you will not believe, surely you shall not be established." [2] But the philosophical root is in the thought of St. Augustine. Before I trace this I want to elaborate the scriptural and traditional notion of faith from the religious standpoint.

"Faith" is frequently used to translate the Hebrew "amen," meaning certainty. The latter word also suggests reliability, loyalty, and trust. Our use of the word "faithful" today carries this same sense, but in the Gospels and Epistles even the noun "faith" sometimes carries the sense of trust. What is less easy for us to sense is that the trust also involved one's being convinced, and, in this case, being convinced of that which is eternally real. And, as the Christian tradition grew, "faith" was also used to refer to the objective content of Christian belief. In this way it developed that "faith" has two sides. Where we are contemplating the object of faith, divine revelation, we speak of "faith that . . ." and this means accepting something as divine. Where we are contemplating the subject or the "existential" side of faith we speak of "faith in . . ."

Each of these two sides has been emphasized by theologians through the centuries. Thomas Aquinas defined faith as "the act of the intellect assenting to a divine truth because of a movement of the will, which is in turn moved by the grace of God." [3] Martin Luther, on the other hand, re-emphasized the nonintellectualistic aspect of faith. For him trust was the most important aspect of faith. For him, too, faith was the trusting in that which it knows to be true. And John Calvin spoke of faith as "a firm and certain knowledge of God's benevolence toward us, founded upon the truth of the freely given promise in Christ, both revealed to our minds and sealed upon our hearts through the Holy Spirit."

These statements require interpretation which we cannot take the space to give, but we must notice in them that, despite the desire to emphasize either side, all of them show the two aspects of trust and knowledge. In modern usage the word "certainty" could be brought in to help cover both these elements at once. Whether this can stand philosophically will be the question to which most of this chapter will be devoted. Even with this very abstract and somewhat crude characterization of faith, we can still see how St. Augustine found expression for it in elements of Platonic and Neoplatonic philosophy. The classical locus for the importation of faith into philosophy is St. Augustine's *Enchiridion* which contains the maxim: *"Nisi credideritis, non intelligetis"*—"Unless you believe, you will not understand."

It is not far from the Pauline "things not seen" to the Platonic realm of being—the place of the permanent, immutable, forms. This realm and the soul, which, according to Plato, is akin to the entities in it, stand in contrast to the world of becoming—the world of our experience, our world of things seen, and the same world which St. Augustine saw to be thoroughly fleeting and transient.[4] And it is not far from the Neoplatonic rejection of this outward world, one of the degenerations from absolute unity, to preference for the mystical withdrawal into the self as the way to the real and good. In St. Augustine's words:

> And being thence admonished to return to myself, I entered even into my inward self, Thou being my Guide: and able I was, for Thou wert become my Helper. And I entered and beheld with the eye of my soul (such as it was), above the same eye of my soul, above my mind, the Light Unchangeable. Not this ordinary light, which all flesh may look upon, nor as it were a greater of the same kind, as though the brightness of this should be manifold brighter, and with its greatness take up all space. Not such was this

light, but other, yea, far other from all these. Nor was it
above my soul, as oil is above water, nor yet as heaven above
earth: but above to my soul, because It made me; and I
below It, because I was made by It. He that knows the
Truth, knows what that Light is; and he that knows It
knows eternity. Love knoweth it. O Truth Who art Eternity!
and Love Who art Truth! and Eternity Who art Love! [5]

St. Augustine's description of his discovery of God contains many of the marks of the classical mystical experience,[6] and it would be very difficult to characterize it
as a rational inference. Moreover, he intimates that it was
only through direct divine assistance that he made the
discovery.

More relevant to our special topic is what was discovered: the Light Unchangeable, Eternity, Truth, and
Love form a unity which is the source of all being and
knowledge, and when one is joined to it in love, he
understands. There is here the suggestion of the Platonic
doctrine that genuine knowledge comes from inner illumination and not sense-experience, and that at the sum-
mit of reality stands the source of this illumination. Let
me now try to clarify these interconnections *vis-à-vis* the
doctrine "Faith precedes reason."

If this passage is about faith at all, it is quite clear that
faith is not for St. Augustine intellectual assent or any
other kind of assent. It is clearly not experience and just
as clearly not the establishment of the truth of propositions. Yet it seems to be all of these. We must acknowledge
that what St. Augustine is recording is unique. It is vision
of the totality at an instant. But in this vision St. Augustine
thought he saw everything in a new light. And with this
awakening of the mind, it clearly follows that truths
known through sense-experience and reason will have to
be seen in the light of what St. Augustine saw in this
vision or they will not be taken aright. These truths do not
have to be grasped in an instant, but as each is grasped
it will have to be related to the scheme implied.

The connection of Truth and Love is perhaps another way of stating this same point. What is known is inseparable from what is loved. The object of knowledge cannot be fully grasped unless it is also the object of love. If, for instance, it is true that God created the world, as St. Augustine believed, and it is also true that it was created from "the will of a good God that good things should be," then the world will have a certain order called for by that will and its object. And if this is not addressed with love, then one cannot grasp the order there to be grasped. Without first responding with love, we can never understand. And, equally, what we understand will be seen to be in accordance with our deepest desire.

Parallel with Plato's view that the making of true judgments is not something we accomplish as the result of anything external to us, St. Augustine believed that all knowledge came from within. But he adds that the individual finds the truth for himself through the guidance of the revealing word of God. We shall return to this point in a moment.

It is important to avoid the mistake of thinking that St. Augustine regarded faith as the sum of presuppositions necessary to rational knowledge. Such presuppositions would be that there is an external world, it has a causal order, and the like. It is certainly true that such presuppositions are made, and, while there is debate over the exact status of these presuppositions, no one would deny that they are required. But that is just the point: everyone holds them and yet only some share St. Augustine's religious faith. To hold that religious faith is a necessary condition of knowledge would be obviously false because nonreligious people have knowledge.

It is nearer the truth to say that St. Augustine was stressing the coming to terms with the knowledge one does acquire, with the directions in which one will continue to search for knowledge, how he will appropriate that knowledge to the living of his life, and how he will interpret it. In his vision St. Augustine saw his place in the scheme of things. He was thus made capable of using knowledge for the living of his life.

This is not very far from the familiar idea that each person has his own special set of beliefs about the world, how things operate, and where he fits in and among them. No one can have a rational grasp of all the facts he needs to live, and so structures a world of how things ought to go for him, and acts. St. Augustine's view is that there is no variety of such structured worlds. There is only one, and until an individual discovers it through faith and lives according to it, he will continue to find himself in one false relation or another to the world. It is even doubtful that any sense can be given to the idea of having all of the facts necessary to live one's life because something besides mere information seems to be needed for living one's life, or so St. Augustine would have us think.

An objection to St. Augustine's thought is that what is reported in the above passage is nothing other than his grasping the interconnections of his own, although implicit, view of the world. What St. Augustine saw was, not that his view was true, but how the parts of it were related, and his view was one which happened to relate the self to everything else. This is the illumination he was talking about, and in this sense we are prepared to speak of illumination even today. But to confuse this with somehow establishing the truth of his view is tantamount to begging the question. For he is saying he who does not see things this way does not grasp the truth.

Another consideration here is that it was not until the time of Descartes (1596–1650) that a sharp distinction was made between the use of reason to support the doctrines of the Catholic Church and the use of reason to establish truths according to reason's own standards. And when we recall that the problem of knowledge had not yet become one of relating the mind and its operations to the external world, we can understand why we have difficulty following St. Augustine.

Part of a reply in support of St. Augustine might be in the realization that at this depth of response to the world it is not clear whether anyone can avoid begging the question. When we speak of how one takes the world, so to speak, there seem to be only two questions. First, is there one and only one way to take it? Second, how adequate is each of the ways of taking it? We cannot but expect that a person who has made his way will insist that his is the correct one. And the very difficult problem of assessing the adequacies of it not only protects him in his view, but also is a reason for his holding fast to it.

Some light on the first question is found in the work of the Danish philosopher and theologian, Søren Kierkegaard (1813–1855). His work is extremely complex and not readily amenable to introductory thoughts. I shall focus on only one, but a central one, of his views—the subjectivity of truth; and, because it is so subtle, I shall discuss it at some length. This is no extravagance given the profound influence Kierkegaard has had upon modern theology, especially quite recent work on faith.

So far, we have seen that, traditionally, faith has two aspects, a specific content and a response to it. We have also seen how, despite St. Augustine's success in fusing certain Greek philosophical elements with Christian belief, the tension present in his view between the two aspects of faith has increased in the development of Western thought. As the idea of the objective world with its uniformities grew, so grew the idea that most, if not all, of our knowledge comes from and is about that objective world, even, in a sense, knowledge of our selves. Our will, hopes and desires, trust, love, and other emotions have nothing to do with what we find and can, if not scrupulously guarded, interfere with our finding the truth. Indeed, our inner conditions are themselves subjects for this dispassionate, objective inquiry because they, no less than planetary motions, are natural phenomena. And things hoped for or not seen are all subjective, and for some thinkers they are merely imagined.

For Kierkegaard these developments do not displace religion. On the contrary, they make the religious problem as he sees it all the more insistent. The question Christianity tries to answer is, What does the individual, the subject, count for? In the ultra-rationally interpreted world he counts for nothing. There the individual, as he tries to understand himself, finds no answer to what he is or what it is to be a subject. Kierkegaard puts the point this way:

> . . . nature, the totality of created things, is the work of God. And yet God is not there; but within the individual man there is potentiality (man is potentially spirit) which is awakened in inwardness to become a God relationship, and then it becomes possible to see God everywhere.[7]

Christianity is concerned with this subjectivity for its truth exists only in subjectivity if it exists at all. Christianity has absolutely no existence in objectivity, and neither has the individual person. And thus the question is not whether to accept Christianity on the basis of its objective truth; that, for Kierkegaard, is paganism. The question is about the decision one makes in gaining faith, and since it is a pure decision, no objective considerations bear upon it. In other words, faith is not a matter of belief.

Another reason is that the object of faith is not something belonging to this rational world. It is, rather, the absurd. Kierkegaard writes:

> Suppose a man who wishes to acquire faith; let the comedy begin. He wishes to have faith, but he wishes also to safeguard himself by means of an objective inquiry and its approximation process. What happens? With the help of the approximation process the absurd becomes something different: it becomes probable, it becomes increasingly prob-

able, it becomes extremely and emphatically probable. Now
he is ready to believe it, and he ventures to claim for himself that he does not believe as shoemakers and tailors and
simple folk believe, but only after long deliberation. Now
he is ready to believe it; and lo, now it has become precisely
impossible to believe it. Anything that is almost probable, or
probable, or extremely and emphatically probable, is something he can almost *know*—but it is impossible to *believe*.
For the absurd is the object of faith, and the only object that
can be believed.[8]

In other words, that which can be cashed into knowledge cannot be the object of faith. The object of faith is
just that which cannot be a matter of belief in the sense
of something which a little more evidence will make into
knowledge. This point is somewhat suspicious and I shall
examine an objection to it later. Now I shall focus again
on the individual side of faith and leave for the time being
that to which he is joined in the faith relation.

The distinction, then, is between the world of univer-
sals, of scientific generalization, and the world of the subject, his inwardness. Where philosophy teaches us to become objective, Christianity teaches us to become subjective, to face our existence and cease avoiding it in scientific generalizations. This is not easy. We are constantly
tempted to fit ourselves into categories, to speak of ourselves in heroic terms borrowed from patterns we have
seen elsewhere. But consider for example what it means
to die. No matter how much information we gather, death
is uncertain. I cannot understand my death, then, as a
mere generality because I am not a human being in general, not a number only, not, say, number 234 of the 383
traffic deaths over Labor Day weekend. This is what my
death may be for others but not for me. Then is there no
way to approach this, my death, because I cannot experience it any more than others can mine or I theirs?

To answer that there is no way for the individual to
apprehend death, if it is to be more than a simpleminded
dodge, it will be necessary to show dialectically, or, putting

it somewhat crudely, rationally, why there can be no answer. But this only takes one back to all the other existential problems, which is where he started. To answer that
there is a way, it will be necessary to show what death is.
How will the conception of it transform a man's entire
life? How can one prepare for it, not the thought, but the
actuality of death? If, as Kierkegaard thinks, the task of
life is to become subjective, then the thought of death
for the individual is not something in general but an individual act. The subject develops "precisely in his active interpenetration of himself by reaction concerning his
own existence, so that he really thinks what he thinks
through making a reality of it." [9]

Something similar goes for immortality. Presentations of
evidence in support of it are irrelevant to the question
which is really subjective. It is a question of inwardness,
and the individual alone can put this question to himself
alone and only by becoming subjective. Immortality is not
proven objectively because objectively it cannot even be
stated. It is the most passionate interest of subjectivity and
its proof lies in this very interest.

It may help to explain these ideas by turning them
around somewhat. For Kierkegaard reality is not in the
"objective" world but in the subjective world where the
process of life takes place, where the person achieves his
selfhood or he does not. This is not material well-being; it
is moral or spiritual fulfillment, much on the order of perfection contemplated in the idea of immortality as *zōē*.[10]
Here is where the highest interest of the individual lies,
where he becomes his true self. This is his reality and he
gives it up for the world of dialectical order at the price
of spiritual death. In the specifically religious respect, it is
the set of decisions one makes for himself forming himself
which constitutes this inwardness, and it leads to fulfillment because the decisions arise from commitment to a
supreme value chosen as one's final goal. In traditional
terms, one acts finding fulfillment in his love of God.

With this brief presentation of the idea of subjectivity, we may now be able to grasp the idea of subjective truth as it contrasts with objective truth. In acquiring objective truth, as one does in the pursuit of scientific knowledge, the knower directs attention away from himself toward an object outside himself. With subjective truth the reverse takes place, and the knower directs attention inward. This is how Kierkegaard puts it:

> When the question of truth is raised in an objective manner, reflection is directed objectively to the truth, as an object to which the knower is related. Reflection is not focussed upon the relationship, however, but upon the question of whether it is the truth to which the knower is related. If only the object to which he is related is the truth, the subject is accounted to be in the truth. When the question of the truth is raised subjectively, reflection is directed subjectively to the nature of the individual's relationship; if only the mode of this relationship is in the truth, the individual is in the truth even if he should happen to be thus related to what is not true.[11]

Then Kierkegaard gives this example:

> Let us take as an example the knowledge of God. Objectively, reflection is directed to the problem of whether this object is the true God, subjectively, reflection is directed to the question whether the individual is related to something *in such a manner* that his relationship is in truth a God-relationship.[12]

If it were not for the last clause of the last sentence in the first passage quoted, one might possibly interpret Kierkegaard as saying just that a person has to have more than objective knowledge of God—namely, he has to have the right kind of personal relationship to God as well. This would pose no philosophical difficulties for us, but it would also leave us no better off than we were before Kierkegaard. For the fact is, we have come to the subject of faith just because it appears to be impossible to have objective knowledge of God.

We come closer to understanding Kierkegaard if we give that last clause "even if he should happen to be thus related to what is not true" its proper weight. For Kierkegaard the important question is how one is related to the object rather than what precisely the object is. Here we have to be careful to avoid facile interpretations. It seems clear enough that Kierkegaard is trying to make us aware of all that is not contained in an objective relationship to the truth. I may assent to the proposition that at least two men have set foot on the moon and would thus be in relationship to the truth, my thought conforming perfectly with what is the case. I may even be able to give reasons for my believing this proposition and they may be the appropriate reasons for one's so believing. But it may be that I could not care less. In that case all of the response of all of those people who make toy rockets and look at the moon often with misty looks of future expectation would be entirely absent from my experience. The question is whether there is anything more to the matter than this, and whether this emotional side is something Kierkegaard is concerned to add to religious faith or whether he thinks the objective truth of God's existence is totally irrelevant.

Kierkegaard has been interpreted both as saying that there is no objective truth about God [13] and as saying there is all of the subjective truth in addition to the objective truth, i.e., as accepting the orthodox Christian beliefs but insisting that becoming a Christian requires more than mere intellectual assent to them.[14]

We cannot enter into the problems of interpreting this difficult thinker, but fortunately we need not in order to appreciate what he adds to the concept of faith. This is that the matter of God's existence is indeed an objective question. It is, though, one for which we can have no conclusive evidence one way or the other. This makes no difference from the standpoint of faith because the far more important matter for the individual is what happens to him when he is called upon to believe that which cannot be known. Kierkegaard says this is what subjective truth is:

> an objective uncertainty held fast in an appropriation-process of the most passionate inwardness is the truth, the highest truth available for an *existing* individual. . . . Thus the subject merely has, objectively, the uncertainty; but it is this which precisely increases the tension of that infinite passion which constitutes his inwardness. The truth is precisely the venture which chooses an objective uncertainty with the passion of the infinite. I contemplate the order of nature in the hope of finding God, and I see omnipotence and wisdom; but I also see much else that disturbs my mind and excites anxiety. The sum of all this is an objective uncertainty. But it is for this very reason that the inwardness becomes as intense as it is, for it embraces this objective uncertainty with the entire passion of the infinite. In the case of a mathematical proposition the objectivity is given, but for this reason the truth of such a proposition is also an indifferent truth.[15]

This is almost to say that there is an inverse relationship between the degree to which the objective truth of propositions is attainable and the importance those propositions have for the existing individual; and paradoxically, that those propositions for which objective truth is flatly unattainable matter most. This means that there will always be in such matters objective uncertainty or, to use a plain word, doubt. This which matters most to the subject, the doubt, rather than turning the subject away from the objective uncertainty, only heightens the passion with which the subject will affirm it. It is this process which Kierkegaard regards so important that he calls it "being in the truth."

Obviously, this is not truth in the favorite sense of the philosophers, by virtue of Kierkegaard's structuring of the entire problem. In fact, subjective truth does not seem to be truth in any straightforward sense, though there seem to be several senses combined which are important enough not to lose by dropping the word "truth." These are senses of "truth" referring to what one discovers about himself as the "object-subject" of self-knowledge. In this context it would be the discovery one makes about what is truly important to him as a subject, the sense of truth when we refer to one's integrity and those matters pertaining to it, and possibly some kind of insight into the nature of individual existence. Certainly those who like to talk of religious truth as a truth of some special kind seem to be talking about various forms of experience or realization of the kinds just mentioned. It is significant that when we deal with these notions in a philosophical context, we feel constrained to draw back from using the word "truth."

Important as this last point is and even though it turns out to be the basis for numerous objections to Kierkegaard and other existentialist thinkers, both religious and nonreligious, it is just here that we get an insight into the modern notion of faith as Kierkegaard's thought has shaped it. Subjective truth is really faith and for Kierkegaard

> Faith is precisely the contradiction between the infinite passion of the individual's inwardness and the objective uncertainty. If I am capable of grasping God objectively, I do not believe, but precisely because I cannot do this I must believe. If I wish to preserve myself in faith I must constantly be intent upon holding fast the objective uncertainty, so as to remain out upon the deep, over seventy thousand fathoms of water, still preserving my faith.[16]

It is only too obvious, one must object, that my relationship to God would not be profoundly altered if I were to have objective knowledge of God.[17] I would, after all, be expected to do God's will, and in all probability I would be as willing to do his will as I am now and perhaps even more willing. My obligation to him for my existence and my desire to worship him in his majesty would not be lessened and the latter would probably be heightened by my direct awareness of his power and the positive evidence of his greatness. If, in short, my relationship to God is really important, then my knowing God directly should not diminish it. But Kierkegaard apparently believes that what is really important to me is none of these; rather, it is what I am called upon to be and do in light of this objective uncertainty that is of highest value to me. It is the spiritual growth required to make the leap of faith that is important to me as a human being, and this is the highest of the spiritual achievements such as trust in one's fellow man, devotion to another or to one's duty or cause, and willingness to lay down one's life for his conviction.

Here the discussion has reached a level where it is not easy to see how the argument is to proceed. We seem to have reached a point, not of reasoning, but of evaluation, of appreciating and weighing certain elements in life and saying "Yes, this is truly more valuable" or "No, it is not." But in the background there is the possibility that Kierkegaard has used a familiar religious thinker's strategy—trying to get us to feel it is religiously appropriate that we have no objective truth about God.

In Kierkegaard's language, what is affirmed as truth in subjectivity is a paradox in objectivity. It is in the contradiction between the subjective conviction and the objective uncertainty that faith is rooted. In the specifically Christian context, we have, instead of the objective uncertainty, a certainty, namely, that objectively we have an absurdity. It is absurd—"that the eternal truth has come into being in time, that God has come into being, has been born, has grown up, and so forth, precisely like any other individual human being, quite indistinguishable from other individuals." [18] This is the absolute paradox. And it is this which philosophy cannot remove and why the man who tries to believe by the use of reason rather than against reason is so comic.

Part of a standard objection to Kierkegaard has already appeared. Kierkegaard's view of the God-relationship is very special indeed, and, though not inconsistent with the biblical understanding of that relation, is still only one part of it. Faith is an important element in this relation, but there are also many other elements. For one thing miracles as discussed in the last chapter are supposed to be very positive evidence for the beliefs of biblical Christianity. For another, some very specific events and situations described in the Bible have added to the complex nature of that relationship.

Another objection is that it is difficult to keep subjective truth distinct from objective truth, no matter what Kierkegaard thinks. I mentioned that the idea of subjective truth is probably a complex of ideas on truth as we apply this notion to the so-called "inner self." But one sure sense is the sense of "true" as it occurs in the phrase "the true self." It is this truth found in self-discovery, when a man finds out what it is truly to be, that Kierkegaard is surely in large part treating. But it is not clear that this truth is really very different from sound psychology. It could be that a naturalistic observer might after all discover objectively what Kierkegaard says can *be* only subjectively. Psychologists, notably C. G. Jung [19] and Rollo May,[20] claim to do just that. I shall have more to say about this later.

Martin Buber, the Jewish theologian, may fairly be called an existentialist thinker working with some of the central Kierkegaard themes. It happens that Buber's starting point is exactly the difference between the two realms we have found difficult to keep separate in Kierkegaard. Consideration of Buber's view here will add to our understanding of faith.

Kierkegaard suggests that we are systematically asking

the wrong questions or heeding the wrong features of our experience in such a way that we cannot grasp religious truth. We are seeking God as an object of experience or inferable from experience when the real relation is not as subject-to-object but as subject-to-subject. God is discovered in the relationship which holds between persons, in encounter and not in experience.

This approach is taken up in Buber's masterfully written *I and Thou*. It is a profound book, in some respects easy to appreciate and in others very difficult. As reading follows rereading, its meaning becomes clearer. It is not the ideal book to try to summarize, but if it is understood that the book itself must be read, then some discussion of it here, especially in this context, should still be helpful.

For Buber the fundamental relation in life is a relation holding between subjects. Each of us discovers in his very first consciousness a developing difference between himself and another self—between I and Thou. This is not the familiar philosophical distinction between self and nonself. It is the consciousness of the self as different from another self, I in contrast to you. Indeed, my awareness of you is not the result of my first becoming aware of myself and then something other than myself. Rather, I am aware of you from the beginning as included in myself, and then gradually the difference becomes more conspicuous. I am aware of you and me from the beginning.

From this awareness of I and Thou as persons I become aware of a world of things, and I and Thou are dissociated from this world. This world is not of persons but of things.

Thus my awareness is first of the relation called "I-Thou." Then it is of the relation called "I-It." These combined words do not name but intimate two *relations*. Each intimates one aspect of man's double response to the world, and the world is thus for man twofold. These two words are both primitive, but "I-Thou" is prior to "I-It." Each marks the self in unity with something else: there is no "I" taken simply. And, though both words are primary, and though both words are combined words, the "I" in relation to objects is somehow less than the "I" in relation to other selves. I can say with my whole being, "I-Thou" alone, not "I-It."

The latter word is the word of science, of experience and observation. The former word is the word of "relation." True, both words intimate relations, but for Buber only the "I-Thou" relation is living, i.e., a relation of life, of living subjects to one another.

In the realm of "I and Thou" there are three different areas. There is, first, our life with nature where we relate to substances in the living relation which is preverbal; where the substances are not categorized, analyzed, or mathematized; where we relate to animals perforce without words. There is, second, our life with men where our living relation is predominantly speech; where we can give and accept "Thou"; where the relation is love, not mere emotion, but the responsibility of an "I" for a "Thou." There is, third, our life with intelligible forms where we think primarily of the work of the creative artist and its meaning for us; where the experience is still semantic in a broad sense but not yet at the level of abstract ideas.

It is at this point where we reach the boundary of the realm of "I and Thou"; for were we to come to abstractions we would have entered the world of "I-It." Thus the realm of "I and Thou" contains, not only preverbal and verbal relation, but superverbal relation as well, where there is not just relation between self and sub-self, and self and self, but self and super-self. We have more than man's loving speech; we have the "mute proclamation of the creature" and the "form's silent asking." In this way all three relations are mutual and reciprocal. For Buber this means the "Thou" is envisaged by the "I" as undivided by categories, and as that which pervades everything in its realm—as boundless in a spaceless and timeless light.

The realm of "I-It," by contrast, is in a very general

sense the world scientifically understood. It is the realm where the space and time coordinates apply; things are measured, analyzed, and brought under causal laws. Moreover, it is the world where men do not encounter and love but relate to what they have made into things by appropriating them to their use. This is where man becomes less than his authentic self and diminishes to a user. In fact, man himself is destined to become an "It" by participating in this realm.

The Thou lessened to an It may find a living relation and become full again. But it is impossible for us to continue in this relation. We as I's have to be users too. It is only that we must not quit the realm of Thou taking the realm of It for our permanent abode. As Buber puts it:

> . . . the moments of the *Thou* appear as strange lyric and dramatic episodes, seductive and magical, but tearing us away to dangerous extremes, loosening the well-tried contexts, leaving more questions than satisfaction behind them, shattering security—in short, uncanny moments we can well dispense with.[21]

And yet, he continues,

> Without *It* man cannot live. But he who lives with *It* alone, is not a man.[22]

This view compares closely with Kierkegaard's view. The world of It is in world of space and time, and thus the world of objectivity. The world of Thou is not in space and time, but in the "Centre" where all living relations meet. Each particular Thou is thus a glimpse into the eternal, the eternal Thou, and each living relation is perfectible only in relation to God, the eternal Thou— pure, absolute, and unconditioned. This I understand to suggest that every Thou is a timeless present which contains or somehow leads to the presence of God, and it is as he relates to the eternal Thou that man finds wholeness.

Each encounter of a Thou with a Thou prepares the individual for this Absolute Relation, relation with God.

The idea of encounter is important for Buber. The word "encounter" has a connotation to be contrasted with many words used in religious discussions to refer to the man-God relation. Encounter is not becoming at one with God, not a loss of self within self, but rather a meeting of two persons, separate but related. It is difficult to say whether man finds wholeness before or after he encounters God. It is clear that Buber does not want us to interpret encounter as the result of withdrawal from the world. This means that life experiences are somehow integral, or preparatory to, encounter.

It is in encounter that we discover God, not in reasoning from empirical evidence or from *a priori* truths, but directly. The three forms of living relation—in nature, between men, and with intelligible forms—are also the three routes to the presence of the Word. Life with men is the most important of these three routes because it is the model upon which we base our understanding of our relationship with God. In this relationship there is both address and true response, and Buber is concerned to show that these aspects of the man-God relationship exist. But God's response is made in the meaning everything takes as the result of our relationship with him.

This last point is not very clear, but to one who would make this objection the reply from the religious side would be that any attempt to analyze this response would be an error. This goes also for the objection that there is no real reason to say that our sense of the world as full of significance is God's response. These are misunderstandings projected from the objective world, the world of It. We do not know what the encounter is from God's side: we know only from our side. It is our will, not God's grace, with which we must concern ourselves. I cannot seek God. I can only wait for the encounter. There is no plan for me to follow to bring about the encounter. Encounter with the eternal Thou is a development of encounter with particular Thous. "If only we love the real world . . . really in its horror, if only we venture to surround it with the arms of our spirit, our hands will meet hands that grip them."

Here is the faith required. Unless we go forth in life in full confidence of its ultimate significance, we will never encounter the eternal Thou. But when the encounter comes, we will be able to know that it is real. Just how we shall know this Buber does not explain, but he says in it "We receive what we did not hitherto have, and receive it in such a way that we know it has been given to us." [23] We are not given the verification of a proposition that God exists. We are given a presence in which we feel "The whole fullness of real mutual action," "The inexpressible confirmation of meaning," and feel that the meaning is not because of another life, as many theologians would contend, but a meaning in this life and this world.

Like Kierkegaard, Buber believes that this meaning can be proven true by each man in the living of his life. This way of putting the idea of proof shows us that Buber is not talking about proof resulting in knowledge. Even the truly religious man can never know the solution to the riddle of the universe. Thus for Buber, as for most modern thinkers on faith, there is an essential agnosticism in faith. The proving true of the religious belief is achieved in action, not in thought. The man so acting and so proving has no grasp of the universe as a purposeful whole. But a man, in living his life as part of such a purposeful whole, will find in himself a fulfillment which confirms, in the sense of justifying, his faith.

This view points to the scientific and practical world of our epoch as a place where there is no room for religion or morality or free will. Buber tells us that there is another mode of experience—that of encounter, of true self with true self. The question I must raise is whether this does not preserve religious thought at the cost of taking it out of the world of experience. Certainly the world of science and economics is also the world of moral obligation and of life decisions. The biological facts of life intrude themselves upon our whole being—upon our interpersonal relationships and upon our life plan.

Religion and science are not in Buber's mind rival world hypotheses, but it is difficult to know just how they cannot be and how religion can yet deal with the so-called facts of life. This same objection would go for Kierkegaard, though he tries to show how what I have called facts of life are not facts of life. We have seen the idea of the whole man invoked in many places, but we have not seen how the Thou is a whole man at all.

This takes us to a second objection against Buber's view. It is difficult to see how the I-Thou experience can be either more than or less than an emotionally moving experience. It has to be something less than the physical and chemical processes now accounting for so much of man's inner life. Of course, it is plain that such things as deciding, wishing, grasping the meaning of, and the like are far from being accounted for physically. But it is just as obvious that such inward operations take place when the agent is using what he knows about the world of It— time, space, and other physical considerations. Is not the reality of God to man something met in these considerations? And if it is, it is difficult to see how the categories of the world of It are utterly inapplicable to God. In short, Buber frees us from the dogmatic assurance of popular religion with an appealing view calling out the highest that is in man, but he seems to do this by repudiating traditional moral and intellectual parts of religious life.

There is something to be said on behalf of Buber here, namely that these objections trade on difficulties faced by the entire philosophical world. I want to come back to this shortly, but after I have spent some time discussing a third existentialist thinker who has also influenced modern thought on faith. This is Paul Tillich.

In his book *The Dynamics of Faith,* Tillich develops the idea of faith as "ultimate concern." Man, as do other beings, has many concerns. But, for man, some of these necessities are spiritual. Tillich means by the latter what we would normally call cognitive, aesthetic, social, and political concerns. Some of these concerns are urgent. Some one of them may be ultimate, in which case it demands complete surrender of the individual who accepts it as ultimate. And he does this willingly because it promises complete fulfillment. For example, the concern may be the preservation and development of the nation, and the individual may be called upon to sacrifice everything for it. Thus the nation is the center of ultimate concern and, for those committed to it above everything else, it is their god.

It is important to emphasize the promise of fulfillment as well as the demand made by the center of ultimate concern. Usually, the promise is not defined, but it is always ultimate fulfillment—a great nation or spiritual expansion. The god of Mammon demands much and promises much, but, after all of the efforts and investments by those who worship him, the promises are not fulfilled.

Faith is more than belief in a certain truth and more than an emotional commitment. It is an act of the total personality, what Tillich calls a centered act. It lies behind all of the individual's undertakings and directs all his acts. Without this centered act all of one's energies become dissipated and his efforts pointless. One has no plan, no program of life, and no center of control.

Because faith is an act of the total personality it contains elements of both the conscious and unconscious self. But the presence of unconscious elements does not make faith an unconscious compulsion. These elements merely join with the conscious elements. Faith is a conscious act requiring decision in the sense Kierkegaard meant it. Faith must be understood as a matter of freedom, not of compulsion—something freely accepted. It reaches to the unconscious because it is so fully embraced. It is the core of one's actions, the center of his disposition to act.

Faith also transcends both the rational and nonrational elements of man. Man is a rational being. But, even in a broad sense of the phrase "rational being," man is more, and not to be identified with the rational character of his mind. Man can decide for or against reason from something beyond his rational and irrational character—the center of his self-relatedness where all elements of his being converge. Again, faith is not either cognitive or emotive but both. It is not just a matter of the will either. It has cognitive and emotive content, and it is an act of will.

Faith stems from concern. As we have seen, some concerns are only relative and transitory. Man's experience centers on such finite goals unless he elevates himself to something beyond. Unless he does transcend them, he will not find fulfillment, and it is this failure of all lesser goals which drives him to the unconditional, the eternal which he can somehow grasp beyond his ordinary experience. It is the infinite which man grasps as ultimate, as what is most significant and enduring almost as a kind of contrast with his own finitude. Thus faith is concern with the unconditional, the passion for the infinite. Ultimate concern is concern about what is experienced as ultimate.

This brief exposition of the *Dynamics of Faith* may help us understand the difference between the traditional sense of "faith" with its emphasis upon the authority of revelation and the more recent existential sense with its emphasis upon the God-man relationship disclosed in encounter. It is important to note that the traditional sense of "faith" did not suggest anything flimsy about religious belief. In fact, faith has the advantage of being based on divine authority instead of human knowledge with its intrinsic fallibilities.

It is fair to say that the certainty of faith has been weakened in modern times. Some of this devolution has been recounted as we have gone over the growing influence of science on the totality of modern thought. But we must not let this interpretation of the course of modern thought, both philosophical and religious, obscure an important fact about the concept of faith. It may be true that faith is now thought of more from the side of the believer than from the content of his belief. The influence of existentialism upon theology supports this proposition. But this change of emphasis which we have observed taking place through several centuries is not necessarily the manifestion of growing theological desperation.

The English word "faith" in early use was specifically religious. Whatever it signified—trust in God or in the truth of revelation—its meaning has to be understood first in a religious situation. Later the word was used in secular situations. So it will not do to look upon the use of the word now as it has been reduced to trust and think that the return to the inward side of faith in theological writing today means that faith is nothing more than a psychological disposition. The emphasis upon the God-man relation made by modern religious thinkers may just as well be construed as a return to a fundamental presupposition which the religious person finds is required to make sense of experience. Just how this issue gets settled is not at all clear. This explains why, despite the tremendous influence of science on modern thought, especially through the technology it affords, the religious person does not acquiesce.

There is another important aspect of this issue. It is sometimes said, even by very sympathetic philosophers, that the existentialist theologians get credit for calling our attention to important psychological aspects of man

*manifest & scientific*

which we are very likely to forget in the modern age. If this were all there were to the matter, then the objection posed earlier, that what these theologians tell us ought to be as readily available to the natural scientist who studies human psychology, would make an end of the matter.

There is, however, something far more profound involved. This is the deep division in all thought today between what Wilfrid Sellars has called the manifest and the scientific images of man.[24] These are two images of man-in-the-world, two philosophical perspectives which appear to clash and which the philosopher must try to bring into harmony.

The manifest image is the framework in terms of which man came to be aware of himself as man-in-the-world—the framework in terms of which man first encountered himself. It is in this encounter that man became man, man forming his self-image and the image in turn shaping him. This encounter of man with himself is a paradox in that man could not be man until he encountered himself. For man to be able to move from pre-conceptual behavior to genuine thinking about himself or anything, he first had to leap to a level of awareness wherein he could see himself as judging, deciding, evaluating. It is this leap which might be taken as the Special Creation.

Now man is located in and can locate himself in an irreducibly new field of awareness. Sellars' contrast between this manifest image and the scientific image of man is not a contrast between a naïve, pre-scientific conception of man-in-the-world and a critical, scientific conception. For the manifest image itself is a refinement of man's "original" image of himself. This image has undergone empirical refinement. All of those canons of investigation which we have come to call "scientific method" have emerged in this refinement process, with one important exception. This is the form of scientific reasoning which postulates imperceptible entities, and principles to them, to explain the behavior of perceptible things.

This image defines one of the poles to which philosophical reflection has been drawn. This includes the great speculative systems of ancient and medieval philosophy and many systems of recent and contemporary philosophy. This includes the existentialists in whom we are particularly interested in this present chapter, but Sellars has in mind all of the other major systems of Continental thought, as well as those major trends in British and American philosophy. Sellars' reason for this is that all of these philosophies may be viewed as offering accounts of the manifest image of man-in-the-world to be taken as an account of what man and the world really are. This may explain why theologians are most comfortable with philosophies of this kind. All of these views Sellars brings under the heading "perennial philosophy of man-in-the-world." Philosophies in the Platonic tradition, taken broadly, center around this notion of the manifest image endorsed as real. This is the large-scale map of reality, and science merely adds more and more detail plus an elaborate technique of map-reading.

The "original image" has undergone categorial refinement, too, in the hands of these philosophies. When we ask what there is in the world according to these philosophies, we get the objects we might expect to be included in the manifest image—persons, animals, lower forms of life and "merely material" things, like rivers and stones.[25] Now the primary objects of the manifest image are persons. This is familiar from Buber, who, going back to the "original image," finds it a world or, using Sellars' term, "framework" in which all objects are persons. Thus the refinement of the original image into the manifest image is the gradual "de-personalization" of objects other than persons.

At this point I want to interject the observation that our faith theologians of this chapter might all be fairly viewed as trying to stop this de-personalization process by focusing upon man's relationship to God as an ultimate personal relationship which, once abandoned, spells the dissolution of the manifest image of man. With this strategy it is made to appear that there must be some truth in the idea of God or, more modestly, in the God-man relationship. This does not follow, however, because the manifest image of man may turn out to be irreducible no matter what one believes about God. But I believe we shall at the end of this discussion be able to grasp the importance of faith in arbitrating our decision for either the religious or the scientific view of man-in-the-world when we see the present state of philosophy and the difficulty of resolving the conflict of the scientific and the manifest images of man.

Returning to the main point, the refinement which Sellars speaks of has been the modification of an image in which all the objects do everything persons do. Indeed, it ceases to be appropriate to say that objects other than persons act. Originally, it would be right to say that the wind blew down one's house, fully implying that the wind decided, or was persuaded, or did it thoughtlessly, or inadvertently. And it would be right, on this understanding, to respond morally to such action taken by the wind. There are primitive remainders of this in our present responses to tornadoes, plane crashes, and tripping over croquet arches. There are also poetic recrudescences of this. But, in general, the refinement meant that natural phenomena were understood less and less as persons and their interrelations, not more and more as impersonal objects, but more and more as truncated persons.

The scientific image of man-in-the-world is also an idealization. It is the image derived from the fruits of theorizing with the postulation of imperceptible entities and their proper principles. It is true that there are as many images of man-in-the-world as there are sciences which have implications about man—man as he appears to the theoretical physicist in a swirl of physical particles, forces, and fields; man as he appears to the biochemist; to the physiologist; to the behaviorists; and to the social scientist. All of these images differ from man as he appears to himself in sophisticated common sense, the manifest image. But the scientific or postulational image may be construed as an integration of these separate scientific images.

Each of the scientific images rests on and is an extension of the manifest image. It might thus appear that the integrated scientific image presupposes the manifest image. This is true with respect to methodology: Each scientific theory is an extension at a different place and using a different procedure from the other scientific theories within the world of the manifest image. But all of them together provide us with what is supposed to be a complete image and thus to define a framework which is supposed to be the whole truth about that within the new image. This new image stands as a rival to the manifest image, and from its point of view regards the manifest image as inadequate.

A great deal has to be said about the integration of the scientific images and the issues surrounding the idea of the unity of the sciences. Sellars says some of it, and we cannot take the time to go into even his remarks. But it should be clear from what has been said so far that the outcome of the rivalry between the two images will have important implications for theology because it will make a definite impact on the amount of seriousness we will be able to give the image of man which faith attempts to preserve and within which it tries to maintain the individual's status as something important in reality.

Obviously the dissolution of the manifest image of man-in-the-world into the scientific image is not in itself an elimination of the content of faith. But it is just as obvious that if the manifest image of man should disappear, the idea of faith, especially as it has been conceived by the existentialist theologians who dominate the field today, cannot even get off the ground. And it is a legitimate criticism, I think, of the existentialist theologians that they do not explore the relationship between these two modes of thought which they are willing, in fact eager, to acknowledge. It is not at all clear how Kierkegaard's objective reality and subjective reality fit together, if at all, or Buber's I-Thou and I-It, or Tillich's conditioned and unconditioned goals.

Sellars sees three possible ways in which these two worlds may be related. The first is to say that manifest objects are identical with systems of the imperceptible particles of the scientific world in the same way a forest is identical with a number of trees. The second is to say that manifest objects are what really exist and the systems of imperceptible particles are abstract or symbolic ways of representing them. The third is to say that manifest objects are appearances to human minds of a reality which is constituted by systems of imperceptible particles.

The first alternative leaves us with the problem of accounting for such things as the pink of a pink ice cube, which, after all, is manifestly a homogenous continuum however small a region of it we take. It also leaves us with the problem of explaining our sensations which, after all, are manifestly not cerebral particles, and to say that they are is really to take them out of our world-picture, leaving it unintelligible how a thing can even *appear* to be colored. Further, it leaves us with the problem of accounting for our thoughts and their introspectable qualities in terms of cerebral processes.

The second alternative is an attempt to put the shoe on the other foot. It tries to do away with the puzzles mentioned above by insisting upon the reality of the objects in the manifest image and the unreality of the postulated entities of the scientific image. It refuses to take seriously the claim of any part of the scientific image to be what really is. Reality is the world of the manifest image. Postulated entities of the scientific world are merely symbolic tools which help us find our way around in the world. These latter entities are not really the names of actual objects or processes. Thus the true philosophy of man is the one which accepts the manifest image, with the scientific image as a mere part of it, a conceptual tool used by manifest man as scientist.

To take the third alternative seriously, we would have to be able to develop an account of how the sensations, images, and feelings of the manifest image could be re-expressed in terms of the scientific image. Now, even assuming that such a feat could be accomplished, and it is far from being shown to be impossible, the reversal of the Platonic tradition would scarcely have begun. For we would still have to show that the categories pertaining to man as a person faced with ethical and logical standards, and, I might add, deeply personal decisions, all of which can and often do conflict with his desires and impulses, are reconcilable with the idea that man is what science says he is. Thus undertaking to reconstruct all of the specifi-cally human in terms of the scientific framework will be met with that whole battery of objections which can be mustered on behalf of free will.

This is not to say that battery would be sufficient to defeat the attempt. But this is not the only difficulty the reconstruction meets. There is a logical difficulty which makes the proposed reduction in principle impossible. In order for me to be able to describe the actions of persons I must think of the person whose action I am describing as a member of my group and he must think of himself in that way. Thus to recognize a creature as a person is to think of it and oneself as being in community. The fundamental principles of community for Sellars are the most general common intentions of that community with respect to the behavior of members of the group. Foremost among these are the ones which make meaningful dis-course possible.

This means that the scientific picture is not completed by finding ways to say all of this in factual statements.

Rather, it is completed by adding to it the language of community. And we can construe the actions we intend to do and their circumstances in scientific terms. In this way we relate the world of scientific theory to our purposes and take it to ourselves so that it is no longer an extension of our world but is itself the world in which we live. We are far from being able to do this, but with this understanding we already transcend the dualism of the manifest and the scientific images.

This abridged, crude, and somewhat inaccurate presentation of Sellars' view of the relationship of these two images does not settle anything, but it suggests a great deal. The views of faith we have considered have been built upon the radical separation of the two modes of thinking of man-in-the-world. It is by taking this separation for granted that they were able to make a case for the position of faith on the grounds that it alone keeps man as he truly is, and then takes this as support for the content of faith because that which preserves man as he truly is must itself be true.

But even if what man is to himself is not identical to what he is for science, does this guarantee that the theologians have the correct view? Surely the failure of a theory does not automatically validate its major opposition.

### Faith and Belief.

It has emerged in the preceding discussion that the concept of faith in modern theology has taken on a special kind of logic which makes it unassimilable to mere belief. Faith has come to mean that which is by its nature not convertible into knowledge and is thus quite unlike belief, which is. For Kierkegaard, it will be recalled, the simple soul who hoped for just a little more religious information so that he could be convinced of the truth of his belief is pathetically comic. There is even the virtue in the Christian tradition of believing without have seen, or having been given direct proof. This is still not quite like what Kierkegaard meant because for him it is not as though one might have been given proof but believed on faith. Rather, it is that there is and will be no proof forthcoming, and that is what is important about faith.

But there are some philosophers who insist that if one is going to believe and act on certain religious ideas, the possibility of the conversion of this belief into knowledge must exist, and there should normally be some evidence, no matter how slim, that the belief is true. Their model of knowledge is something like this:

1. One must believe that the proposition in question is true.
2. The proposition in question must in fact be true; otherwise, the believer could legitimately be made to retract his claim to know.
3. The believer must have available to him what might be called proper grounds for believing that the proposition is in fact the case; otherwise, we would be able to rule it a mere coincidence of his belief with what is the case.

We can see, then, that the existentialists' notion of faith is quite unlike belief because they hold that doubt is ineliminable from faith. When we take into account the historical background to the unfolding of this existentialist view, it seems not entirely off the mark to suspect that it is at least in part because there is no evidence of any satisfactory kind that the view has developed at all. With the weakening effect our consideration of the contrast between the manifest and the scientific images has had on the *prima facie* appeal of the modern notion of faith, it becomes important to look once again at the situation of believing without conclusive, or even supporting, evidence.

This is precisely the situation William James takes up in his well-wrought essay "The Will to Believe." Although there are very close affinities between James's thought in that essay and Kierkegaard's thought, James is there directing his attention to the view that it is intellectually disreputable to believe that for which there is not sufficient evidence. James argues that under certain circumstances there is nothing contrary to the canons of reason, nothing intellectually corrupt, in believing without evidence—provided, of course, there is no evidence to the contrary. And he thinks that believing in God is just such a situation.

The circumstances which make belief without sufficient evidence acceptable pertain to the decision to act or live according to a certain proposition or not. This is the option. The *first* condition is that the option must be living, not dead, i.e., either of its alternatives must be a real possibility for the person trying to decide. For most of us the option to become a snake-worshipper is not living and thus unlike our living option either to continue as conventional members of our society or to drop out. The *second* is that the option must be forced. It cannot be avoidable. This means that I must do something with respect to the choice-situation. I cannot just walk away from it as I can from the option of buying cotton candy. The *third* is that the option must be momentous, not trivial—something affecting the course of my life or the whole quality of it. James's example is dramatic: whether to leap across a glacial crevasse to follow the only path to safety and, in doing so, take a very high risk of one's life; or to cling to the far side and freeze to death because one does not have proof that he will make the leap successfully. The resemblance to Kierkegaard and Buber should be obvious.

James thinks that our option to believe in God or not meets all of these conditions. Like Pascal he thinks that the gain of believing, should it turn out to be true, would be very great, and the loss, should it be false, is trivial. Unlike Pascal, though, James thinks the importance of the choice lies not in some promised afterlife, but here in this life. Typically, belief in God has the immediate benefits of enabling one to face life optimistically and with the confidence that life is worth living and the good life worth pursuing. "Faith in a fact can help create the fact," James adds. Belief in God and all of the benefits he would bestow itself helps create those benefits. With this kind of positive value coming from believing, it is neither intellectually corrupt nor psychologically pathological to believe if one has the will to believe.

One could respond to James with most of the objections brought against the existential theologians—generally speaking, that they had not considered how precariously the manifest image of man hangs on future developments in scientific and philosophical thought. But from another standpoint, one should, I think, take the point as a more modest response to the crisis of faith in the modern age with the conclusion that, from where we stand now and until there is evidence against religious belief or such belief is shown to be incoherent, there is nothing in the ethics of belief, so to speak, which rules against it. And when we consider the immediate value to us of such belief, if there really is any, we should go ahead with our belief.

This way of leaving the matter may put faith in a much more tentative position than theologians are accustomed to put it and certainly more than the religious person would like it to have. But from the philosophical point of view there is no other way than to take this guarded position. Until there is some resolution to the status of the manifest image of man or, even more dramatically, some way of seeing what faith might be, or whether it could be, should man become totally interpreted scientifically, this rather general position of James is still the strongest one a person can take for the sake of faith. It is certainly stronger than founding faith exclusively on a view of man-in-the-world which might suddenly crumble in the floods of new information about man and the universe.

## Psychological Dimensions of Faith.

Since the influence of Sigmund Freud on modern thought has declined, there has been little of significance in recent years on the psychology of religion. Not more than two decades ago the relationship between psychology and religion was eagerly discussed. It has been said of the theologians discussed in the last section that a major part of their achievement is in bringing forth important psychological considerations pertaining to religious belief. This should not be denied. But it should be clear from the last section that this achievement is far less significant in light of the deep division in thought with which these theologians were contending. The central problem of these theologians was not psychological at all: it was metaphysical. They have tried to show us that there is an understanding of ourselves which cannot be undertaken within the scientific framework.

These considerations suggest that it would be helpful to take up the psychological bearings of faith and the psychological critique of faith at this time. This juxtaposition will help us to put faith and the psychological critique of it in perspective.

There is one aspect of religion and psychology we shall not deal with, and this is the relationship between mental health and being religious. From the philosophical standpoint, it makes no difference at all about the authenticity of religion if people who believe are also happy. We are too familiar with technical ways of inducing blissful psychological conditions to take very seriously such therapeutic claims on behalf of religion. Of course, if it could somehow be shown that there is absolutely no way to happiness except through religious belief, this might be enough to make us consider it. But even this would not be enough to establish the truth of the belief. It may be correct to say that religion, even as an illusion, has great importance to a person. But philosophically we are committed to such a frame of mind that discovering something is an illusion is enough to make us reject it.

There is another side of this particular relationship between psychology and religion which counts against religious belief in the philosopher's eyes. This is the apparent power of psychology to explain why people are religious, how they came to be, and why they continue to be. There is an important distinction to be made and for philosophers of religion to insist upon. This is the distinction between the psychological processes underlying certain beliefs and the truth of those beliefs. Moreover, we train ourselves to accept true beliefs whether we would like them to be true or not.

Freud begins his famous book, *The Future of an Illusion,* by taking note of this distinction. He continues, however, with what he thinks is a psychological explanation because, as he says, he will not prove or disprove any religious beliefs, but, when he explains their psychological foundations, we most certainly will not want to believe them.

Freud begins with the generalization that in all cultures it is necessary to squelch certain instincts. A mass of unsatisfied instincts, what Freud calls frustrations, is generated from the prohibitions all cultures set forth to insure their continued existence. And these prohibitions cause privations. There are certain privations which affect everybody. These are the oldest ones stemming from the prohibitions of the earliest cultures. Their effect was to detach these cultures from the primordial animal condition of mankind.

The prohibited instinctual wishes Freud has in mind are incest, cannibalism, and murder. These wishes are still strong in us today, as is evidenced by the present need for prohibitions against them. Further, where there is no fear of punishment these instinctual wishes are fulfilled. These acts are still performed.

That which is peculiarly religious in a culture begins

when the hardships of life of the individual become apparent in the culture. In general, the individual and all mankind find life hard to endure. The individual's culture imposes some privations. His fellow man makes him suffer despite the numerous laws of the group. And he suffers from natural evils—floods, earthquakes, and famine, all of which give him pain—and finally he must die. The result is that a great deal of anxiety develops within the individual.

He reacts to the cruelty of his fellow man by becoming resistant—by responding with hostility. But there is little within his own means he can do to defend himself against the supremacy of nature—all of the forces which threaten him and, ultimately, death. Man's self-esteem is seriously menaced and craves consolation for a life in a universe filled with terrors. But the culture does not abandon him: it provides a defense for him.

Here, according to Freud, those ideas we recognize as specifically religious begin, and the humanization of nature takes place. Man cannot cope with impersonal forces and with fate, because they are too remote. He has no means of affecting them. But if the elements have passions like our own souls, we can relate to them and feel closer to them. By thinking of all things as full of spirits, we are no longer entirely defenseless. We can exorcise, appeal, and bribe the forces of nature. Perhaps we are not defenseless even against death. At least, we can react psychically to it. Relief of our anxiety and even the hope that we might master our fate are gained.

With the rise of science and all it implies for our understanding of the forces of nature, the universe loses its human or anthropomorphic traits. Man is still helpless as he is. His desire for protection, an infantile desire which Freud calls "father-longing," still remains. Thus God still has a function. Through our relationship to God we might yet exorcise the terrors of nature, and reconcile ourselves to the cruelty of fate, especially death. And God

can make recompense for our sufferings and the privations imposed on men by communal life. There is a re-
ward somewhere, somehow for sexual abstinence, etc.

With the rise of science there is also a shift from gods
as the lords of nature to mere creators. This is the common understanding of Deism. Only in miracles do the
gods interpose themselves upon the workings of their
creation. They do this to show that they are still lords of
all. But even among the ancients there were intelligent
men who began to wonder who was in control, and this is
shown in their putting fate even above the gods. Thus it
fell to the gods to adjust the evils of culture.

All of this, then, arises from the need to make tolerable
the helplessness of man, and it is built from material
offered by memories of helplessness in childhood. It takes
two directions. First, there is help against the danger of
nature and fate. Second, there is help against the evils of
human society. Life in this world serves a higher purpose.
We do not know the purpose, but it is understood to be
the perfecting of human nature. Perhaps the human soul
will achieve perpetuity. No matter, there is no need to
worry. Everything is planned by a super intelligence. Its
will is inscrutable, but ultimately we shall see that it
cares for us. Providence is really benevolent and is only
apparently severe. This is the path of the monotheist.

Freud's argument is that religious ideas have arisen
from the same need as all other "achievements" of culture
—culture's need for defending itself against the crushing
supremacy of nature. Man might have destroyed himself
or dissipated his energies in frantic responses to his anxie-
ties. Religion offered control and a basis for sanctions of
the moral code needed for the preservation of culture.
The religion was offered as a divine revelation. This is an
integral part of the working of religious systems.

Religion consists of certain dogmas, assertions offered
as facts, and authentic descriptions of reality. They purport to tell the individual something he has not discovered

himself, and they admonish the individual to believe the dogmas. But the basis of this admonition is peculiar. In the case of all nonreligious propositions, we expect and train others to expect reference to observation, either direct or indirect, and we require that the observer leave his personal convictions aside and adopt an attitude of tentativeness, even to that which he thinks he has seen to be the case.

This is decidedly not true with regard to the grounds of religious dogma. The attitude taught is that they deserve to be believed. An example of what Freud has in mind is in St. Paul's words: "This is a true saying and worthy to be received: that Christ came into the world to save sinners." [26] We are told to accept the articles of faith because our ancestors did, because of evidence merely inherited and because it is forbidden to question their authenticity at all.

This cannot but arouse suspicion. There can be only one motive for this different way of treating religious claims: society knows very well their uncertain basis and covers it. And since the claim that they are divine revelation is itself a religious dogma, it too is under question. It, as well as any other claim, cannot bear its own proof. Freud concludes:

> Thus we arrive at the singular conclusion that just what might be of the greatest significance for us in our cultural system, the information which should solve for us the riddles of the universe and reconcile us to the troubles of life, that just this has the weakest possible claim to authenticity. We should not be able to bring ourselves to accept anything of as little concern to us as the fact that whales bear young instead of laying eggs, if it were not capable of better proof than this.[27]

From here the attempt to support religious belief becomes, in Freud's eyes, a series of desperation moves. Here, for example, is where spiritualism enters. One seeks in the idea of survival after death to be able to establish at least one article of religion as free of doubt. But these alleged phenomena have not been properly verified. They are more likely the product of the would-be believer's own mind. And, as we have seen in the discussion of immortality, if certain phenomena of spiritualism should be established, we are still a long way from having proven that there is such a thing as human immortality; farther still from having shown that this has anything whatever to do with religion.

Another desperation move is in the high-handed assertion, *"Credo, quia absurdum est,"* I believe because it is absurd, from the great Christian writer Tertullian (c. 155–after 220). This we have encountered in Kierkegaard. Religious doctrine is outside reason's jurisdiction because it stands above reason, somehow. The truth of religious doctrines must be inwardly felt. Freud dismisses this as of interest only as a kind of voluntary confession, not as a strategy with intellectually binding force.

A third desperation move is to recognize religious doctrines as groundless but to behave "as if" they were true. This is a move made from a variety of practical motives. We should, according to it, behave as if we believe these fictions were true. Freud says this is not a compelling view. It is also the source of spiritual corruption because people working with it believe it allows them to continue acting exactly as if it were true.

Thus these dogmas do not result from experiences or reflection. They are illusions, "fulfillments of the oldest, strongest, and most insistent wishes of mankind. The secret of their strength is in the strength of these wishes."[28]

Infantile helplessness is terrifying. The infant needs protection. This comes through love supplied by the father. Without a father and with the helplessness still felt, we cling to a belief in the existence of a father. This father is a more powerful one. In Freud's earlier work, *Totem and Taboo* (1918), Freud saw the infantile need expressed in admiration for the father but matched with hatred for the father because of the child's desire to have his mother and other women sexually. He would slay the father, eat him, and take the women; and this complex desire arouses a sense of blood guiltiness. Out of this guilt two taboos emerge—no incest and no murder. Transferred to the more powerful father, this guilt is traded in return for protection.

This happens when religion in the form of totemism has the totem as a father-substitute. Here the covenant is made with the father. There will be no incest and no murder, in turn for protection, care, and indulgence. Thus the totemic system arose through the filial need and sense of guilt. Later religions can be understood as having this same basic nature, but varying with the degree of civilization in which it lives. The Christian communion is a rehearsal of this guilty deed. This has to go on because it is neurotic behavior. While this neurosis is universal, it is still considered neurotic by Freud because guilt is not natural to man. It is not very clear what "natural" means here.

In *The Future of an Illusion* Freud is concerned more with the intellectual manifestation of the neurosis. This is in the harboring of an illusion, which must be distinguished from a delusion. A delusion is something necessarily false. We must remember that Freud is not making so strong a claim against religious doctrine as to call it false. And, in fact, illusions, like dreams, could come true. The poor but honest country maiden could really be carried off by the prince. But she harbors an illusion because, in expecting a prince for no good reason, wish-fulfillment is a prominent factor. A belief is an illusion when there is a disregard for its relation to reality.

Why not believe if we so desire, then? Even Freud, along with the other skeptics, admits that the statements of religion cannot be disproved by reason. Freud replies,

> Yes, why not? Just as no one can be forced into belief, so no one can be forced into unbelief. But do not deceive yourself

into thinking that with such arguments you are following the path of correct reasoning. If ever there was a case of facile argument, this is one. Ignorance is ignorance; no right to believe anything is derived from it. No reasonable man will behave so frivolously in other matters or rest content with such feeble grounds for his opinions or for the attitude he adopts.[29]

Belief without grounds is insincere and intellectually dishonest. Philosophers stretch the meaning of words and make "God" some vague abstraction and pose as believers. They pride themselves on having attained a higher and purer idea of God when, in fact, they have merely emasculated the mighty personality of religious doctrine. Others say a man is "deeply religious" who senses his insignificance in the universe, but in Freud's eyes this is irreligious in the truest sense of the word.

Finally, the psychological examination of religion has revealed religion as illusion. We know when and by whom religious doctrines were formed. Now we see the motivation for their formation. And it should appear strange that religious doctrines turn out to claim just those things to be the case that we in our weakness want to be so. This much recognition cannot but suggest that the future of the religious illusion is very doubtful indeed.

We have not gone into Freud's thought in any depth to justify a close critique of his view on religion. We must restrict our attention to certain general objections which can be made apart from the psychological theory upon which Freud based his remarks on religion. One very obvious starting point is that, theory or not, there is insufficient evidence for anyone to offer a full account of the origins of religion. Take for example the key step in Freud's account—the humanization of nature. He does not make it very clear just how this happened, even though he believes he knows why it happened. But how it happened is important—whether, say, the world was always grasped anthropomorphically or whether only gradually.

Some authors discussed in this chapter would disagree with Freud saying nature always was anthropomorphically interpreted. And there does not seem to be any easy way to settle the matter.

That Freud himself is prepared to set aside the question of the truth of religious doctrines helps draw the distinction between the philosophical scrutiny of religion and the psychological, sociological, or any other type of examination of religion. There is a difference between the causes of religious belief and the truth of them. Suppose that many, most, or all religious beliefs do stem from man's basic wishes. The question of the truth of those beliefs would still have to be settled. Freud points to the coincidence of wish and belief. True, this is very strange—there being "just so" answers to our deepest doubts. But, on the other hand, it is no less odd to think of the universe and our life in it without some of these answers coming to mind. The very idea of existence is difficult to contemplate without the mind's straining to account for the mystery in some way.

Freud stakes a great deal on the idea that religious belief comes about through the infantile father-longing. The criticism of religion implied by this idea may hold against some or all of Western religions, but it does not hold against the religions which have no father-image. Of course, even with Western religions there is a good question whether Freud has correctly interpreted the role of God.

These rather negative remarks against Freud's view of religion should enable the reader who has been over the preceding chapters to see that Freud has left a great deal out of consideration. There has been a very long history of reasoning about religious doctrine and seeking its foundations. Most of it has been honest. There has been a long and complex history of religion, and only some of it falls comfortably under Freud's speculative theory.

C. G. Jung (1875–1961), in his book *Psychology and*

*Religion,*[30] takes a considerably different attitude toward religion. Even though his view of religion is not radically different from Freud's view, Jung's attitude toward religion is far friendlier than Freud's. Jung's interest in religion comes from his hypothesis of the collective unconscious and of the primitive archetypes which are its contents.

Jung's very great emphasis on the collective unconscious is part of the major difference between him and Freud, which centers on the interpretation of the libido. The collective unconscious is "the precipitate of humanity's typical forms of reaction since the earliest beginnings." [31] Jung finds a connection between meanings found in modern symbolism, which is apparently spontaneous, and ancient theories and beliefs. Since there is no historical connection or conscious tradition in these cases, Jung believes that the continuity between these forms of symbolism can be accounted for only by there being an unconscious continuity among men.

This continuity does not consist in the unconscious transmission of ideas. To claim that it did would be very difficult to make out because of the tenuousness of the evidence of many historical connections among peoples. What Jung has in mind is an inherited form something like the ability among men to produce the same or similar ideas over and over again. As Jung puts it,

. . . the connection of modern symbolism with ancient theories and beliefs is not established by the usual direct or indirect tradition, and not even by a secret tradition as has often been surmised. The most careful inquiry has never revealed any possibility of my patients' being acquainted with books or having any other information about such ideas. It seems that their unconscious mind has worked along the same line of thought which has manifested itself, time and again, within the last two thousand years. Such a continuity can only exist if we assume a certain unconscious condition carried on by biological inheritance.[32]

This possibility Jung calls the "archetype."

Jung does not explain the status of these archetypes. He seems to think of them as models for psychological exploration, and he does not want to assign to them a specific metaphysical status. He wants to leave them open for empirical investigation. Unfortunately, it is not clear what empirical investigation would be in this case.

More important, no matter how Jung's investigations would proceed, there is no way in which they would lead to the substantiation of religious doctrines. Jung himself does not mind this. He is content to call them "psychologically true." And in a line of thought quite contrary to Freud's, he writes,

> Religious experience is absolute. It is indisputable. You can only say that you have never had such an experience, and your opponent will say: "Sorry, I have." And there your discussion will come to an end. No matter what the world thinks about religious experience, the one who has it possesses the great treasure of a thing that has provided him with a source of life, meaning and beauty and that has given a new splendor to the world and to mankind. He has pistis and peace. Where is the criterion by which you could say that such a life is not legitimate, that such experience is not valid and that such pistis is mere illusion? Is there, as a matter of fact, any better truth about ultimate things than the one that helps you to live.[33]

Then Jung goes on to explain:

> This is the reason why I take carefully into account the symbols produced by the unconscious mind. They are the only things able to convince the critical mind of modern people. They are convincing for very old-fashioned reasons. They are simply overwhelming, which is an English rendering of the Latin word "convincere." The thing that cures a neurosis must be as convincing as the neurosis; and since the latter is only too real, the helpful experience must be of equal reality. It must be a very real illusion, if you want to put it pessimistically.[34]

For Jung inquiry into religion is examining the inter-relations of the archetypes and determining the function of religion. He believes that function is the integration of the psyche, and he believes this is the important thing about religion, not whether its content is the truth about ultimate things. For, he reasons, "no one can know what the ultimate things are." [35] If the healing power of religious experience can make life healthier and better in all the other respects, then one can regard this as God's grace.

Anyone who has followed this chapter so far will be able to supply the relevant philosophical criticism. Has Jung escaped its force? If he has, it would seem to be only because he and his followers have already given up on the question of the truth of religious doctrines. Jung does not concern himself much about the differences among religions, even though we have seen that there is a mean-ingful, if crude, evaluation procedure for choosing among them. In fact, Jung's notion of the collective un-conscious works toward integrating all religions. Cer-tainly, *it is against the tradition of religious thought to equate religious faith with individual satisfaction.* A reli-gious person may achieve peace through some religion or other, but there is a very important difference between say-ing this and saying that the worth of religion lies in its mental health-giving properties.

The entire Jungian religious enterprise serves as evi-dence of the decline in the weight given to genuine reli-gious thought. It is true that Jung's view still carries the aura of the manifest image of man in the world and this is, no doubt, part of its appeal. But it is also the attempt to lend scientific credit to traditionally religious things. This indicates that the scientific framework has gained the upper hand. Combined with Jung's total skepticism about genuine religious knowledge, it is difficult to avoid the conclusion that, no matter how interesting it is, its chief merit regarding religion is in allowing people to go on talking and thinking as if little or nothing has been changed by the advent of science in modern thought.

Although this approach to religion is still prepared in its own way to take seriously the religious experience of orthodox believers, it is not unlike more recent attempts to find and cultivate something in the world which cannot be devoured by scientific categories. I have in mind the recent increase in interest in astrology, witchcraft, and the occult. This is not to put Jung's contribution on the same plane, but to say something about the popular appeal it has. To drop the truth of religious doctrine from consideration, no matter how good the reason, is to blend readily into the landscape of popular religion where the need for belief outweighs attention to the truth.

It is the difficulty any modern man of reflection has in taking seriously anything, no matter how desirable, which he knows to be an illusion. It is almost as if there is something dearer to him than any cherished belief and that is the truth itself. He cannot consciously belie what is appropriately called illusion, and all of the great religions would discourage him from doing so.

This should help us see something more about the nature of faith. Comparing two great psychologists with three great existentialist theologians has shown us that under the concept of faith falls a great deal more than emotion.

# IV

## Religious Experience

### *Introduction.*

To anyone who has read the preceding chapters keeping in mind their historical direction, their sequence might appear to tell the story of the decline of religious experience. They began with traditional theism, an outlook in which God lives and acts among us, and in which the existence of God so pervades thought that everything that is and happens is related to him. They ended with serious critiques of this outlook and what could be interpreted as desperate attempts to save it by performing certain logical twists on the very fact that there is no such thing as evidence of knowledge which can appropriately be called religious.

There has been, however, a recent resurgence of interest in religious knowledge. A number of philosophers have come to think that the canons of science have been rather too widely applied with the result that people have come to regard forms of thought other than scientific forms as totally vacuous. In this overextension of scientific canons many traditionally accepted sources of knowledge—not just religion—have become discredited merely because they were not scientific. Certain philosophers assumed that there was only one form of knowledge, the scientific, and any other form was either pre-emptible by science if it contained any knowledge at all or else it never did contain knowledge. Recently, philosophers have tried to look more closely at these other forms to see if, taken seriously and in their own terms, they may not be sources of genuine knowledge.

It is clear, however, that no matter what these investigations reveal there will always be special difficulties associated with claims of religious knowledge. There is something to the familiar idea that a God fully known is no longer God. Faith would be eliminated and with it the spiritual values and the sense of mystery it affords. But this is not the central issue. We could still respect God's authority, find other ways to personal fulfillment; and we could be satisfied with the stimulation of what is yet to be known. Nor is the fact that religious claims always imply something beyond the realm of normal experience the central issue, even though that is an issue.

The central issue is that religion, unlike other alleged forms of knowledge such as historical and aesthetic, does not have obvious authenticating procedures. It is always forced back upon itself, as Freud noted,[1] to insisting upon some kind of self-authenticating status. It is fair to ask why God does not reveal himself directly instead of through his prophets or miracles. But it is not clear how this could be done. Almost anything one can think of to serve this purpose would be immediately given over for scientific explanation. Indeed, many well-meaning religious people have been very pleased to find possible scientific explanations for certain miraculous phenomena such as the appearance of the star of Bethlehem and the gift of manna in the wilderness.

Direct revelation would not in itself be convincing. Just as a miracle does not exist in and by itself but in the interpretation put upon it and the significance assigned to it in a proper framework and with the necessary presuppositions made, so religious experience in general requires criteria of authenticity. For, if something is to fall outside the scientific framework, then it must be subject to judgmental procedures. Otherwise, one cannot tell, especially in the case of so-called religious experience, whether he has known something or has merely sported with madness. A person may claim to have seen God, but the rest of us want to know how he and we could tell it was God.

In raising the topic of religious experience we want to understand what it is supposed to be. This is even preliminary to understanding its authenticity. We are not interested in the emotions of religious experience. Certainly what goes by the name of religious experience may be very moving to those who have it, but, important as this is, it is not our main concern. We might say that religious experience, so far as it has philosophical interest, has two parts or, possibly, is of two kinds. There is the emotional element or experience which people have in religious contexts or attribute to religious causes. There is also the cognitive element or experience which reveals something to the person who has it. It is what William James calls *noetic*.[2]

Religious experience is also more than just a matter of directly apprehending God. Our investigation of this topic is more than whether people, most notably mystics, directly apprehend God. Religious experience must not be too narrowly conceived or else we risk losing what may be most interesting about it. We are interested in knowing whether something may be learned through religious experience. For example, in religious experience an individual may discover certain things which indicate to him a deeper meaning to the world, or tell him something about his own life, or serve as evidence, perhaps even very indirect evidence, of God and his relationship to this life. Certainly such knowledge has been claimed to come from experience typically taken as religious.

The knowledge is supposed to be something like that we have when we say we know there is someone in the room, though we have not seen, heard, or been told there is; or that the woman in my dream was my sister, though I have no real sister to recognize in the dream and no one in the dream told me she was my sister. In this second example, my saying she was my sister is stronger than my saying I had the feeling she was my sister. There are dreams about suspecting or feeling that something is the case. But this is one where I know, in the context of the dream, that this is the case. The religious person is claiming to have somehow experienced, not dreamed.

### Religious Knowledge.

C. B. Martin [3] objects to the idea of religious knowledge which has the form:

> I have direct experience (knowledge, acquaintance, apprehension) of God.

Therefore, I have valid reason to believe that God exists. There is nothing to warrant this inference, he finds. The premise is an abstract formulation of the variety of claims Martin labels "psychological," such as

1. I feel as if an unseen person were interested in (willed) my welfare.
2. I feel an elation quite unlike any I have ever felt before.
3. I have feelings of guilt and shame at my sinfulness.
4. I feel as if I were committed to bending all my efforts to living in a certain way.

These state my complex feelings and experiences, but, no matter how unusual they may seem to me, nothing follows from them except, perhaps, that I have them.

Just as there is no deductive relationship between such psychological claims and the existential claim "God exists," there is no inductive relationship between them either. If someone says "I had a direct experience of God at 6:37 P.M., May 5, 1939," we cannot regard his statement as empirical because we have no way to check its truth, there being no agreed-upon tests for distinguishing genuine from nongenuine experience of God. What would we look for in the person's behavior that would indicate that indeed he had seen God? Anything he says or does carries us no further than being able to say that he thinks he has seen God—certainly not to the point where we can say that he must have seen God.

There does not even appear to be any set of qualities such that, upon being shown that they belong to a certain experience, we could say truly this was an experience of God. Any experience of yours which you call experience of God I can have and yet deny it is experience of God. Those who refuse to accept this point, according to Martin, fall back upon saying something like this: "You could not have had my experience and at the same time sincerely deny God's existence." But this, of course, makes your experience an experience of God virtually by definition—something to the effect "Whenever I see or have a certain feeling X, that is experience of God." This is not very convincing.

A familiar attempt to avoid these difficulties is for theologians to claim that religious experience is not sense-experience at all, and that there is a special religious sense which is a unique form of cognition in men. Unfortunately, efforts made to describe this form of cognition rely heavily upon metaphors drawn from other senses and turn out to be quite feeble. For example, it is often said that we "see" the Holy, the Numinous, the Divine,[4] and the idea is one associated with "seeing" a logical connection or something's dawning on us. These locutions suggest a clarity marking certainty and conviction. But there is an important difference between the religious seeing and

the logical: The latter has an external checking procedure and the former does not. Anyone who has made the
mistake of thinking he is dead right on a mathematical
problem knows very well how deceptive feelings of certainty can be.

This consideration alone does not show there is no
special religious way of knowing. Religious knowing may
not be deductive, inductive, or intuitive, but it may still
have its own status. Theologians have often claimed that
it is unique and incommunicable, meaning that it is
something that a person who does not have it cannot
imagine, because it is describable in no terms but its own.
Such a person is like a blind man trying to understand the
experience of light or the sensation of blue. Unfortunately, this only shows that one has no knowledge of these
sensations unless he has them. It may be that we must have
religious experience in order to know what it is like, but
this in no way shows the religious experience is the apprehension of God or proof that God exists.

No doubt the believer has experience which the unbeliever does not. But normally when one does not have
the direct experience of one sort or another, he can have
indirect evidence of what the experience is supposed to
indicate. A blind man, for example, can gather information about the light source producing the sensation of
blue in the man of normal vision. Thus the analogy between the blind man and the unbeliever breaks down.
There is nothing "out there," so to speak, for the unbeliever who does not have religious experiences to try to
detect.

Of course, the theologian can insist on the unique experience itself, making it constitute all the difference between knowing God and not knowing God. But this move
merely equates God with religious experience, so that
knowing God is merely having certain experiences. This is
almost admitting that we have no knowledge of God.
Without relevant tests, anyone claiming to have experi-

ence of God is unable to get beyond his own experience of
the moment. He cannot prove to anyone what he saw and
even he cannot be sure that what he experienced was real.
He can say "It looked to me to be real," but he cannot
prove that it was real.

The religious person wants to say that this is all he
needs: religious experience carries its own guarantee. For
him the religious statement "I have direct experience of
God" is quite different from the statement, say, "I see a
star." The question is, Just how different can it be without
its being nothing more than a statement about the
complex experiences of a religious person? As we have
already seen, the type of statement we acknowledge to be
like this is the guarded statement of the form "I seem to
see . . ." or "It appears to me to be . . ." And statements of
this form are guarded because they contain no commitment about what exists, only about the observer's experience. Obviously the final judge of the truth of guarded
statements of this kind is the person making the statement.
Only he knows for sure what his experience is, and he
knows it in a way which makes the testimony of others
unnecessary.

Now the religious person cannot put his statement on
the same ground as these guarded statements without
giving up his existential point. He wants to claim that he
knows something, the existence of God, by means of his
experience. On the other hand, he cannot or does not desire to put his religious statement on the same ground
as a mere existential statement without any reference to
the experience itself. The experience of God typically
leads to religious attitudes of obeisance and worship. The
person who has knowledge of God is expected at some
time to have certain complex emotions and feelings associated with worship, prayer, and personal encounter. Thus
the religious statement is neither a full-fledged truth claim
nor a purely subjective report.

But, just as the existence of God cannot for this reason

be derived from religious experience, so the nonexistence of God cannot either. When, for example, I say, "I see a book," from this alone nothing at all follows about whether or not I am actually seeing a book. I certainly could be reporting truly what I am experiencing, but whether or not there is a book in my presence is another matter, not entirely unrelated, but by no means conclusively determined by my experience. The same holds when I say, "I see God" or "I am in the presence of God." For surely the religious person wants to hold there is a difference between delusive and veridical experience of God. Religious literature abounds in accounts of false appearances of God, mostly the work of Satan. And it is plain to us that experiences which compare extremely well to religious experiences can be induced by means of drugs. So when someone says seriously that he sees God, he packs in more than just an introspective report. It is worth adding here that some of the religious claims of drug users are subject to the strictures Martin is laying out against statements of religious experience in general. I shall have more to say about this in connection with mysticism.

It should also be clear that the special perceptive powers of religious people carry us no further in establishing God's existence. The man who claims to see what the rest of us cannot may indeed really be seeing something. But, for all he or the rest of us can tell, he may be having hallucinations. His experiences by themselves do not establish that there is anything beyond those experiences. In order to go beyond experience to something "out there," some kind of independent checks are needed. Martin says that ontological reference is something which must be earned.

There is an objection to Martin's insistence on relevant tests as certifying claims of religious knowledge. God may not be the sort of being subject to tests the way physical objects are. God may not be the sort of being which can be pointed to, or pushed or pulled, or weighed or smelled. In fact, most people think of God as a being which, whatever he may be, is not corporeal. In reply Martin says it may well be that God is not subject to tests for the existence of physical objects, but it cannot be that he is subject to no tests for existence. So, if our experiences of God should not be checked by procedures relevant to physical objects, then what sort of checks should be used?

Even so, there is another objection, one not so easy to meet. If religious-knowledge claims must be subject to checks—and here we might be quite thankful to Martin for pressing this point because of what he has shown us —then what about the claims that we must make in reporting the tests? Martin seems to be getting us off on an infinite regress by insisting that all knowledge claims must be subject to checks outside a certain immediate experience prompting the claim. He objects to religious claims because they do not imply relevant checks. But, to make this objection stick, he has to say that all knowledge claims must imply relevant checks.

Now we are asking about what happens when we make a check. Do we not seek further immediate experience which should be attainable given that the original claim is true? Do not our claims reporting the checks then themselves have to be subject to external checks? And if they are not, then are these not instances of self-authenticating knowledge? Further, it seems that unless there are instances of self-authenticating knowledge, we shall never ascertain the truth of any claim, and this is manifestly false since we do have knowledge. Finally, if we are forced to admit some self-authenticating knowledge, why not allow from the beginning that religious knowledge is such knowledge?

Martin might just press the central point that religious-knowledge claims are entirely without connection outside the mind of the self-alleged knower. With other knowledge claims there is at least the move to checks, self-authenticating or not. But this will not do. Unless he can make the self-authenticating point stick, he cannot substantiate his criticism of religious knowledge. For religious claims have extremely elaborate interconnections. This has been made amply clear in the discussion of miracles. Martin himself gives this quotation from the great Spanish mystic, St. Teresa (1515–1582):

> I could not believe that Satan, if he wished to deceive me, could have recourse to means so adverse to his purpose as this, of rooting out my faults and implanting virtues and spiritual strength: for I saw clearly that I had become another person by means of these visions. . . . Neither the imagination nor the evil one could represent what leaves such peace, calm, and good fruits in the soul, and particularly the following three graces of a very high order. The first of these is a perception of the greatness of God, which becomes clearer to us as we witness more of it. Secondly, we gain self-knowledge and humility as we see how creatures so base as ourselves in comparison with the Creator of such wonders, have dared to offend Him in the past or venture to gaze on Him now. The third grace is a contempt of all earthly things unless they are consecrated to the service of so great a God.[5]

The least familiarity with Christian teachings shows how deeply embedded in doctrine and biblical experience are these reflections in which St. Teresa tries to determine the correct source of her profoundly moving experience.

Thus it appears that anyone who wants to make out a case against religious knowledge must look elsewhere for defects. The error of pressing self-authentication as a defect in religious knowledge can be compensated for if, instead of insisting upon final tests, one insists upon the corrigibility of all knowledge claims. I mean by this that no test or checking procedure is to be taken as final. Every knowledge claim we make, whether it is religious, non-religious, or one made in check of these, is subject to correction should reasons develop to make us change our minds about it.

This is not a general skepticism with regard to all knowledge, introduced to save religious knowledge. Knowledge claims can be established because they can be checked out. But no checking out is itself beyond question, and, should the occasion arise, we might well want to look over our checking procedure too. This must check out with certain other truths we hold, and we might in some cases get back to fundamental presuppositions and decide to accept or reject certain claims according as they fit in with our overall understanding of experience.

This way we rid ourselves of the problem of self-authenticating knowledge by denying there is any such thing. The matter of religious knowledge now turns on whether its claims have connections outside the moments of their occurrence, and that they have is obvious from the passage quoted from St. Teresa in which she fits her experience into a whole framework of thought. Even that we can begin to sort out certain experiences as religious or not is proof that these religious experiences have qualities linking them to one another. St. Teresa would have been prepared to throw out some of her experience as delusive had it not met certain conditions established by the framework of her thought. The real question is whether another person will adopt a framework of thought similar to hers.

It thus comes to be much as it was with miracles. It is a matter of how we will understand the world. If we choose to interpret everything which happens in it according to presuppositions which preclude God as a source of phenomena, then we will reject miracles. The same is true of religious knowledge. The argument against religious knowledge is not that it cannot be self-authenticating, nor that it has no external checks, but that it does not square well with the preconditions for interpreting experience set down by those committed to a world view designed to accommodate only physically based phenomena.

There is a familiar philosophical distinction between the context of discovery and the context of justification of knowledge claims. C. B. Martin's main point has been that most theologians spend a great deal of time discussing the context in which religious discovery with its attendant emotions is made and little time discussing the justification of what is supposed to have been discovered. Theologians are too preoccupied with the psychological goings-on to see the important logical considerations. We might add that this is suffering from a pre-modern notion of knowledge.

But the real problem is fitting together the religious and the nonreligious interpretations of experience, or, at least, seeing if they will go together. Some think there is no framework of interpretation and justification of religious experience. As the nonreligious framework becomes more and more extensive and it becomes easier for us to resolve our isolated experiences in its terms, the religious framework deteriorates. This seems to be what has been happening.

Most views of man's awareness of God which attempt to relate this awareness to man's total awareness of the world take the opposite approach. God is not grasped isolated from the rest of experience, at least not the ordinary person's religious experience. Rather, according to John Hick, whose view I shall now discuss, the ordinary religious person ". . . claims instead an apprehension of God meeting him in and through his material and social environments." Hick continues,

> The believer meets God not only in moments of worship, but also when through the urgings of conscience he feels the pressure of the divine demand upon his life; when through the marvels and beauties of nature he traces the hand of the Creator; and he has increasing knowledge of the divine purpose as he responds to its behests in his own life. In short, it is not apart from the course of mundane life, but in it and through it, that the ordinary religious believer claims to experience, however imperfectly and fragmentarily, the divine presence and activity.[6]

The believer's awareness of the divine is mediated through awareness of the world. The idea of mediated knowledge,

Hick says, is not special to religious experience. It is a common and accepted feature of cognitive experience.

According to Hick, there is a certain basic characteristic of human experience which he calls "significance." There is also a correlative mental activity he calls "interpretation" by which significance is apprehended. Interpretation occurs with each of the three main types of existence or orders of significance—the natural, the human, and the divine. We relate ourselves to each only by "a primary and unevidenceable act of interpretation." This act, when directed toward God, is traditionally called faith. Hick's view would thus attribute a cognitive aspect to faith. The object of religious knowledge is unique, but its epistemological pattern, with only certain peculiarities attributable to the uniqueness of its object, is the same as that of all knowing.

Significance, for Hick, is our sense of a "world" as opposed to a mere emptiness or chaos. Because we have this sense, our world is familiar, intelligible, and we feel a part of it. "Significance" used this way implies that our consciousness is essentially consciousness of significance, the taking in of the distinct features of our world as parts of that world.

Interpretation, for Hick, has two senses—one as we speak of an explanation; the other as we speak of recognition or attribution of significance. The former is an answer to the question Why? The latter is an answer to the question What? These two senses are closely related, and in the unique case of the universe as a whole the distinction between explanation and recognition disappears. The universe has no wider context in which an explanation might place it. So it can receive explanation only in the perception of its significance. Thus in this case interpretation is both recognition and explanation. This is why the theistic response to the world is a metaphysical explanation of it.

There are interpretations which are mutually exclusive,

for example, *vis-à-vis* a single object, "That is a dog" and "That is a fox." Only one can be right. But there are interpretations which are compatible, for example, *vis-à-vis* a single object, "That is an animal" and "That is a dog." Both may be correct. This is important to remember in considering the central problem which is to see how religious experience relates to other types of experience.

Significance is essentially related to action. An object is significant to an individual according as it makes a practical difference to him. But the significance of an object is not something which the object merely has: it has significance in a situation. This Hick defines as "a state of affairs which, when selected for attention by an act of interpretation, carries its own distinctive practical significance for us." [7] A person may be involved in many different situations at the same time—as, for example, when he is involved in a chess game, in the company of friends, at the seashore, on the North American continent. There is a whole interlocking mass of these and other situations, and at the most comprehensive level of all is the situation of being in the presence of God within the sphere of an ongoing divine purpose. Again, our problem is how this relates to the lesser situations.

Hick finds three main orders of situational significance corresponding to the threefold division of the universe— nature, man, and God. First, there is our objective environment whose character and laws we must learn and follow in order to survive. Second, superimposed on it, is the realm of human relationships in which we find ourselves responsible agents under moral obligations. Relating ourselves to the moral world is not distinct from relating ourselves to the natural world. It is a particular way of doing so. Third, there is the realm of the divine in which we relate ourselves to God. Even this relating is not distinct from the task of directing ourselves within the natural and ethical spheres, and, indeed, it would be impossible if it were.

Religious significance is, as has been said, the believer's experience as a whole. It is gained through an act Hick calls "total interpretation." He explains this by means of an example.

> I enter a room in a strange building and find that a militant secret society appears to be meeting there. Most of the members are armed, and as they take me for a fellow member I judge it expedient to acquiesce in the role. Subtle and bloodthirsty plans are discussed for a violent overthrow of the constitution. The whole situation is alarming in the extreme. Then I suddenly notice behind me a gallery in which there are batteries of arc lights and silently whirring cameras, and I realize that I have walked by accident onto the set of a film. This realization consists in a change of interpretation of my immediate environment. Until now I had automatically interpreted it as being "real life," as a dangerous situation demanding considerable circumspection on my part. Now I interpret it as having a practical significance of a quite different kind. But there is no corresponding change in the observable course of events. The same phenomena are interpreted as constituting an entirely different practical situation. And yet not quite the same phenomena, for I have noticed important new items, namely, the cameras and the arc lights.

Next Hick asks us to imagine another situation:

> But let us now in imagination expand the room into the world, and indeed expand it to include the entire physical universe. This is the strange room into which we walk at birth. There is no space left for a photographers' gallery, no direction in which we can turn in search of new clues which might reveal the significance of our situation. Our interpretation must be a total interpretation, in which we assert that the world as a whole (as experienced by ourselves) is of this or that kind, that is to say, affects our plans and our policies in such and such ways.[8]

This is what the monotheist's faith-apprehension is like. God is the unseen person dealing with him in and through his experience of the world. It is an interpretation of the world as a whole as mediating a divine presence and purpose. This primary religious perception is not a reasoned conclusion or an unreasoned hunch that there is a God. It is an apprehension of the divine presence within the believer's human experience—not an inference to a general truth, but a "divine-human encounter." It is, besides a way of cognizing, also a way of living. Seeing the world as ruled by a divine love placing infinite value on each man suggests a way of living unlike that suggested by seeing the world as a realm of chance where each man's interest stands against that of the others.

It should not be difficult for any reader to transfer many of the objections to theism studied in earlier chapters to Hick's view. There are two very conspicuous weaknesses. The first shows in the difference between the two imagined instances. In the first instance we have no difficulty imagining the meeting of revolutionaries and what it would be like to discover the photographers' gallery. This gives us the idea that we can do something comparable with the entire universe—that somehow, unseen, there is God's gallery. Now certainly theism requires such a gallery, but it is only an illusion that we can really imagine it and, more important, that such a thing is consistent with our present understanding of the universe. The photographers' gallery lies outside the movie set, but not outside the physical universe. Hick is not out to justify theism and so should not be expected to explain this required transcendence. He is concerned to explain how religious belief relates to our understanding of the world and our life in it. But the question remains, Has Hick really explained anything about theism as long as he relies on an impossible analogy?

The second weakness is in Hick's idea of cognition which he also wants to call interpretation. We can understand the necessary interaction between cognition and interpretation: what we perceive is in part, at least, dependent upon our modes of interpretation. But linking the two, as he does here, only makes it unclear whether we detect the presence of God in our experience or whether we interpret our experience in such a way that it will accord with the divine presence. To choose both of these does not seem to be saying anything.

Hick adds that the theistic believer cannot explain how he knows the divine presence *is* mediated through his human experience. He just goes about interpreting his experience in this way, even though he cannot prove logically that God exists. But this heightens the difficulty. The objection was that it was not clear whether the theist apprehends something in experience suggesting to him the theistic interpretation of his experience, or if he is committed to interpreting his experience in such a way that it will conform to his belief in God. We can agree with Hick that no individual's experience develops along such easily distinguishable lines, but to say that the theist just does interpret his experience that way is not even to attempt to answer the question. More important, this is to dodge all of the questions of why he does, why he continues, why other people do not, and whether he should continue to think in theistic terms.

Hick prefers the mystery. He regards all cognition as unresolved mystery. There is no explanation of how our sensory phenomena constitute an objective physical environment for us. There is no accounting for the real world we know and inhabit, no way of showing it is real. The same is true of our social experience. We just find ourselves to be responsible beings under moral obligations to one another. But even if this is how it is, the manner of interpretation is, though not exactly a deliberate or arbitrary choice, still subject to our intellectual scrutiny. The theist may find himself interpreting his experience in a certain way, because he was brought up to do so or has found it in some way satisfactory, but this does not relieve him of the intellectual responsibility of standing up for its adequacy. I do not say he has to be able to convince anyone beyond the shadow of a doubt, or to be able on command to offer a justification even to himself. But I do say the burden is there, just as it is on the atheist, to defend his ground rationally.

These matters are only ancillary. They are offered only to show up the weakness in holding that theism is just a way one sees and interprets his world. For he has gone about interpreting his world in a specific way and this is either adequate or it is not, whether or not he has been following the majority of mankind in doing so and whether or not he has done so consciously.

There are those who seek to avoid all of these difficulties in religious experience. They do not base their claim to knowledge of God on his presence being mediated through ordinary experience. They claim to know God directly by breaking through ordinary experience. These are the classical mystics whose experience we turn to next.

### Mysticism.

There is a doctrine that at least some men can have direct knowledge of God, not through experience of things or persons and not through reasoning, but through immediate contact with God. This contact, sometimes called intuition and other times insight, is what we shall study as the mystical experience. Mystics are those who claim to have had this experience and who cultivate it in various ways.

Unfortunately, mysticism is frequently confused with many other beliefs. This is partly due to the etymology of the word "mysticism," and partly due to the tendency of the popular mind to lump all spiritual things together. It will be necessary, therefore, to start with a clear statement of what mysticism is supposed to be and then to show how it differs from ordinary experience. In doing so, I shall rely on an authoritative and sympathetic account by W. T. Stace.[9]

We want to know what the mystical experience is. It is

easier to begin by saying what it is not than what it is. It is not something mysterious in the sense that it is enigmatic. Nor is it a form of irrationalism in the sense that it stands against reason. Only in a very special sense is it beyond the scope of the understanding. This means it is not any form of the occult, i.e., those arts and practices using incantation, divination, and other forms of magic. It is also not parapsychology in the common use of that word, i.e., not telepathy, telekinesis, clairvoyance, or precognition. It is often confused with all of these, but it is none of them.

A more understandable mistake about mysticism, but a mistake all the same, is the linking of voices and visions with the mystical experience. Socrates, Mohammed, Moses, and Joan of Arc had experiences of this kind. Their experiences were in different ways experiences of God, but they are not, for reasons which the reader will be able to supply, instances of the mystical experience. It is true that many people who have had the typical mystical experience have also had visions and heard voices. But these mystics warn against confusing the two experiences, claiming that they are not the same. Evelyn Underhill, the outstanding authority on mysticism, says this:

> . . . Ruysbroeck, St. John of the Cross, and St. Teresa herself in her later stages—distinguish clearly between the ineffable Reality which they perceive and the image under which they describe it. Again and again they tell us with Dionysius and Eckhart, that the Object of their contemplation "hath no image": or with St. John of the Cross that "the soul can never attain to the height of the divine union, so far as it is possible in this life, through the medium of any forms or figures." Therefore the attempt which has sometimes been made to identify mysticism with such forms and figures—with visions, voices, "supernatural favours" and other abnormal phenomena—is clearly wrong.[10]

The mystical experience is formless, shapeless, colorless, odorless, and soundless. A vision or a voice is sensuous as is all our visual and auditory imagery.

According to William James, the mystical experience is a new kind of consciousness different from the consciousness wherein our sense-perception and reason are contained. It is entirely unlike everyday experience and wholly incommensurable with it. Ordinary consciousness has three levels. First, there is the level of physical sensations—sounds, smells, and touches. Second, there is the level of images—something like mental copies of sensations such as visual and auditory imagery. Third, there is the level of abstract thought and the reasoning process. Each of these levels has what James calls attendant desires—our responses to the experiences.

Mystical consciousness is different. It is more than just outside the range of ordinary human consciousness. It is not the arena where experiences of ultrahigh frequency and infrared occur. Experiences of this kind are still sensation, whereas mystical experience does not belong to any level of ordinary consciousness. This in part explains why the mystical experience is said by mystics to be ineffable. Language in its normal use is an integral part of ordinary consciousness and so applies only to ordinary experience. It is no good beyond ordinary experience, and this means that the mystical experience cannot be described literally. It may be hinted at in rather indirect ways and the attempts to get at it are almost always very poetic. And, just as the sensuous is excluded, so also must be the conceptual. There is no thought at all involved in the mystical experience.

James finds four distinguishing marks of the mystical experience. It is important to notice that these marks are not features to be discovered in the experience itself, not part of the content of that experience, but something we can say about it. The first is *ineffability*. This is a negative mark. Individuals who have had the experience say that it defies expression. Its content cannot be put in words. We have already seen why they say this. If they are right, there is no way to find out about the experience except by having it oneself. In this respect, James adds, the mystical experience is more like a state of feeling than a state of the intellect. Unless one has had a certain feeling, say of seeing one's child greatly pleased, no amount of talk can give it to him. The second mark is the *noetic quality* of mystical experience. Mystics say the mystical state is also a state of knowledge, an insight into truths unexplored by the discursive intellect. They call them illuminations and find them important and authentic even when gone, despite their ineffability.

The next two characters are less definitive of the mystical experience than the previous two, but they are, James says, usually present. The third mark is *transiency*. Mystical states do not last long and one lasting half an hour or more is rare. They leave memory traces, though, and this will be a central consideration in our evaluation of the mystical experience. The fourth mark is *passivity*. There are certain things one can do to bring on a mystical state, such as fixing the attention and certain bodily exercises, but once the state is achieved, the mystic feels his will is in abeyance and he is held by a superior power. And when the experience is over, this influence does not end: it has worked an enduring change upon the subject.

James does not take these marks as cutting a clean circle around a field known as the mystical experience, and we should not either. They are meant only to help us focus upon a group of experiences in which it is alleged that a common core is discoverable. This may be a challenge even to the most open-minded because the topic is something they may have no notion of whatever. But there is so much written and so much reported about this extraordinary range of experience that we can hardly do it justice by stopping here.

A survey of the literature of mysticism suggests that a certain kind of experience has occurred throughout history and that it occurs even today. It has occurred in all parts of the world and among mystics of various religions. According to Stace, there is a concurrence among mystics

that all fully developed mystical experiences are appre-
hensions of an ultimate nonsensuous unity in all things,
a oneness or a One. This completely transcends ordinary
consciousness, and, in doing so, achieves a unity in which
the distinction between the seer and the seen, or the
knower and the known, completely disappears.

Again, according to Stace, Hindu and Buddhist mystics
agree with the pagan philosopher Plotinus that "We
should not speak of seeing, but instead of seen and seer,
speak boldly of a simple Unity for in this seeing we neither distinguish nor are there two." This experience is
typified by such expressions as "oneness," "unity," "un-
differentiatedness," "God," and "Nirvana."

The Upanishads comprise the main theological docu-
ments of ancient Hinduism which elaborate the mystical knowledge found in the Vedas, the sacred scriptures of Hinduism. Most prominent is the pantheistic doctrine that in all things, but foremost in each human soul,
the supreme, impersonal Brahma or Atman, the World
Soul, is manifested. This doctrine is very properly called
pantheistic because pantheism is the belief that God is not
something beyond the universe and man, and our reality
is only a manifestation of God.

According to the understanding of mysticism contained
in the Upanishads, the undifferentiated unity apprehended
in mystical experience is "the Self." This is because the
mystic has, in ascending to his mystical state, drained his
mind of everything else, everything drawn from experience in this reality, leaving only the self. This self is
identical to the Universal Self. So it is said. This follows if
indeed this is the direct encounter of the transcendent
reality which is the pure self with that of which it is a
part, the Universal Self. Presumably the individual self is
itself part of the transcendent reality, and, once stripped
of its contents drawn from the mere manifestation of the
transcendent reality, it would be known, in some sense of
"known," to be at one with that transcendent reality.

This experience of pure consciousness is usually characterized as being both positive and negative, as something and nothing, as a fullness and an emptiness. It is a state in which one feels nothing, knows nothing, and is left with nothing but a sheer emptiness. At the same time it is pure peace which is beautiful, joyous, and blissful. Frequently, this opposition of positive and negative is expressed symbolically. Light and darkness are frequently mentioned in mystical writings. The famous Spanish mystic, St. John of the Cross (1542–91), wrote a poem called "The Obscure Night of the Soul" which contains these stanzas:

> Blest night of wandering,
> In secret, where by none might I be spied,
> Nor I see anything;
> Without a light or guide,
> Save that which in my heart burnt in my side.

> That light did lead me on,
> More surely than the shining of noontide,
> Where well I knew that one
> Did for my coming bide;
> Where he abode might none but he abide.

> O night that didst lead thus,
> O night more lovely than the dawn of light,
> O night that broughtest us,
> Lover to lover's sight,
> Lover with loved in marriage of delight!

In them are manifested both the light symbolism and the sexual metaphor common in Christian mystical verse.

We find similar imagery in the verse of the English poet, Henry Vaughan (1622–1695). His poem "The World" begins like this:

> I saw eternity the other night
> Like a great ring of pure and endless light,
>   All calm as it was bright;
> And round beneath it, time, in hours, days, years,
>   Driven by the spheres,

> Like a vast shadow moved, in which the world
> And all her train were hurled.

There is also in these lines the idea that, after the mystical experience, the world of ordinary consciousness is perhaps not insignificant, but obviously something small.

Similar imagery is found among other mystical writings. The Tibetan *Book of the Dead* in Mahayana Buddhism speaks of the "clear light of the Void." The Christian Neoplatonist, the Pseudo-Dionysius, speaks of "the dazzling obscurity which outshines all brilliance with its intensity of darkness." [11] The image of darkness is also frequently exchanged for absence or nothingness. Thus the thirteenth-century Christian mystic of Germany, Meister Eckhart, says, "God is pure Nothingness, a desert, a wilderness." The other side of the paradox he leaves implicit —that God is, of course, ultimate reality.

Related to this idea is that the denial of all attributes comes closer to characterizing what is experienced in the mystical state than any attribution. This is the *via negativa* of the Pseudo-Dionysius employed by St. Thomas Aquinas in seeking to isolate in some way the Divine substance. To say of it that it is something or other in a form of predications such as "X is . . ." is to impose a kind of limitation upon this substance which has no limitations. Thus we see in the thought of the mystics something which may be clearly associated with the thought of the philosophers. This point will become more significant presently.

With this necessarily crude and abbreviated characterization of what is supposed to be the mystical experience, we can now turn to some of the implications for religion should there indeed be such a state. In the first place, we should note that, if there is such a thing as mystical experience, it is bound to be associated with certain religious beliefs. There are many who deny that there is any necessary connection between religious belief and mystical experience. This is not a proposition we shall be able to examine. But all religions in a measure as they purport to relate man to something beyond ordinary consciousness, to something transcendent, appear to be dealing with the same thing the mystics are.

It is true that the Western religions—Islam, Judaism, and Christianity—have to reject the notion of undifferentiated unity so frequently mentioned in reports of mystical experience. For them this notion is not orthodox and is properly regarded as heretical. They are theistic and so insist upon a clear distinction between creation and creator. Although creation and men in particular resemble the deity, they are not part of the deity. To say so would be to espouse pantheism. Since most Oriental religions are strongly pantheistic, there is no difficulty from them in the notion of unity. It is interesting that Christian mystics often use the metaphor of sexual union to characterize their experience. This metaphor preserves separate identities in a most intimate relation.

Also, the claim that they have encountered God directly in this life and yet continue living is taken among Christians with rather mixed emotions. It may be putting it too strongly to say that it is unorthodox, but it is embarrassing. Those who claim to have experienced God are claiming to have cut short the arduous path of Christian suffering, sacrifice, and morality leading to spiritual development and final salvation. Yet the orthodox Christian cannot but feel some encouragement upon receiving a report of the divine presence.

There is also the matter of the spiritual purity required to achieve the mystical experience. This is a matter we shall consider later, but we can observe here that many mystics believe their experience cannot be achieved unless they first accomplish a certain spiritual purification which may be effected by various means. It is sinfulness which obscures to men the vision of God and the unity of all things. On the other side of this thinking, there is the idea that a certain kind of holiness of living follows the mystical experience. It is often taken as a kind of guarantee of the authenticity of the putative mystical experience that this kind of living does follow. These, then, are some of the ways in which religion and the mystical experience bear upon one another.

Now I want to turn to several philosophically negative remarks often made about mysticism. The first one appeared already in noticing the difference between the Western and Oriental treatment of the mystical experience. This has to do with the problem of understanding the mystical experience both for the mystic and those who take him seriously. This is simply the problem of interpretation. We find some mystics saying that in the mystical state they become at one with everything else in the undifferentiated unity. These are usually those who come from religions of pantheistic cast. At the same time we find other mystics saying that in the mystical state they are not at one but in union either with God or with everything else. Yet the experience is supposed to be ineffable.

We might well accept certain variances in the reports given the supposed ineffability of the experience, and, after all, how different persons react to the same thing understandably depends a great deal on their frames of reference. But the question does impose itself upon us: how can the alleged fact of the mystical experience count as the objective reality it is made out to be when it is so flexible under the influence of previously accepted religious beliefs? Moreover, some writers on Buddhism are fond of saying that the mystical contact known as enlightenment is not with a deity but with truth about life. While it is difficult to make sense of how something can be both supernatural and not supernatural at the same time, we can still understand that there may well be an experience one might classify as mystical which is not of ultimate reality and not so ineffable as to be without implications for living.

These reflections suggest that the mystical experience

has been too rigidly classified both by those who have had it and those who like to write about it. Of course, it is possible to place emphasis upon experiences of the most abstract sort and characterize these as mystical experience proper. But what produced this set of rather confusing results is the belief that the mystical experience is a unique phenomenon outside the jurisdiction of rational principles and thus safe from the usual embarrassing questions which the average religious claim has to face.

Also, there is the point made very effectively by Bertrand Russell that pushing the mystical experience outside the framework of the ordinary tests for truth only results in cutting the experience from any possible ties with reality as we understand it. We see again the whole range of difficulties raised by Martin in connection with ordinary religious experience in the previous section.

But what about the certainty and convergence of opinion of mystics? Russell counters this by saying that it is only to be expected that similar experiences would occur given the uniformity of the physiological changes usually required before the mystical state is achieved. Fasting, abstention from external observation, and the use of certain drugs produce similar psychological effects in different individuals. Often people become very emotional and deranged when suffering from the effects of these activities. Russell's move is to construe mystical experience as a deviance from ordinary experience but wholly understandable in it.

Let me expand two points from Russell's view of mysticism. First, Russell explicitly mentions the use of drugs as a means of inducing the mystical state. In what I take to be a cynical tone he says,

We all know that opium, hashish, and alcohol produce certain effects on the observer, but as we do not think these effects admirable we take no account of them in our theory of the universe. They may even, sometimes, reveal fragments of truth; but we do not regard them as sources of general wisdom. The drunkard who sees snakes does not imagine, afterwards, that he has had a revelation of a reality hidden from others, though some not wholly dissimilar belief must have given rise to the worship of Bacchus. In our own day, as William James related, there have been people who considered that the intoxication produced by laughing-gas revealed truths which are hidden at normal times. From a scientific point of view, we can make no distinction between the man who eats little and sees heaven and the man who drinks much and sees snakes. Each is in an abnormal physical condition, and therefore has abnormal perceptions.[12]

In more recent years the relationship between drugs and the mystical experience has been more closely examined. Houston Smith has given rather careful consideration to the subject and he concludes that, even though there is no such thing as the drug experience *per se*—since each drug experience is an admixture of the drug, the individual's psychological makeup, and the social and physical environment in which the drug is taken—nevertheless, cases occur in which it is impossible to distinguish between mystical experiences judged authentic which were achieved by holy exercises and experiences which were induced by the use of drugs.

This would seem at first glance to suggest that Russell is wholly correct in his conclusions: it is a matter of chemistry and natural psychology. To this a drug mystic might object that this is merely the inference of one who has already made up his mind about the limits of consciousness. Russell seems to have anticipated this when he writes:

Normal perceptions, since they have to be useful in the struggle for life, must have some correspondence with fact; but in abnormal perceptions there is no reason to expect such correspondence, and their testimony, therefore, cannot outweigh that of normal perception.[13]

This seems to leave Russell with a slight advantage. But this is not the end of the matter.

Whether or not there are chemical causes of the religious experience does not make that much difference. Where Russell seems to have the edge is in the point that what we will in the end count as authentic is that which will fit in with a more or less effective thought system—one which will enable us to manage in the world. But Russell also is most ungenerous in what he allows mystical experiences, chemically induced or otherwise, to be. Mystics have claimed that they have in their mystical experiences discovered for the first time what existence is really like. And in recent years those claiming religious import for drug-induced experiences point out that they have through the use of drugs come to re-evaluate their goals and the goals of the communities in which they live. They say often that they have seen through or beyond the very limited goals of men. If they are right, and it seems to me they could be, then are they not more closely engaged with reality than Russell's rather sober scientifically minded types?

A point made by Smith in connection with the drug experiences is that the drugs seem quite capable of producing religious experiences, but that they do not seem capable of producing religious lives. That is something the person himself must cultivate. Drugs might give him just the experience he needs to free himself from the ordinary in such a way that he can do something rare and fine and even saintly. Here, again, we seem to come back to what *might* happen as the result of the mystical experience no matter how it was induced.

Russell admits that certain discoveries might be made in this state just as they well might be made in a drunken state. This would be only accidental. The mystic might well lay emphasis on how he has been transformed as the result of his experience. The quality of the life lived afterwards is often taken as an indication of authenticity of the experience. This would seem hard to resolve, especially since it is always open to the pro-mystics to say of anyone who thought he had a mystical experience who nevertheless lived rather badly that he did not really have it. Thus the so-called test would only be a tacit decision to say one had a genuine mystical experience only when he becomes saintly. But we have already seen that what results in behavior after a religious experience cannot count as a test of its authenticity. Usually, the nondrug mystic has worked so hard and lived in such a way in order to achieve his experience that the probabilities are rather high that he will continue to live well afterwards.

The second point emerging from Russell's discussion of mysticism is that one might well classify the mystical experience along with many other psychological experiences known as the conversion experience. These are certain overwhelming experiences caused by various things, often a close encounter with death or other feelings of total helplessness, after which one decides to change his way of living. Again, what one does will depend on how he interprets his experience. But if he chooses to interpret it as an intrusion of God into his life, there is nothing Russell has said which rationally blocks his doing so.

Only if one accepts Russell's implicit notion of the struggle for life and his rather severely limited Victorian picture of life, will one think his mystical experience useless. On the other hand, this merely is to acknowledge that the door is still open for interpretations of certain experiences as mystical. It by no means shows that the mystical experience is really contact with God. And, I should think, the foregoing considerations ought to make one very skeptical indeed about mystical experiences.

Finally, we return to the point of interpretation. It would seem that if the mystical experiences on record were as ineffable as some writers would claim, there would be no interpreting them at all. The fact is that they have a character; they are, though tenuously, connected to ordinary life in the sense that having them has implications for the life of the person who has them. Perhaps with less anxiety over preserving the mystical experiences from rational consideration, we might find it possible to resolve some of the puzzles about mysticism and at the same time see that it is a proper continuation of ordinary experience with direct consequences for this life. Just as with miracles, its very possibility lies in whether or not we decide *a priori* so to interpret all our experiences that they must always be explained away. To cut mystical experience completely away from ordinary experience is surely to leave it as nothing more than a quaint curiosity.

### Religious Language.

In now turning to religious language, we are not dropping the discussion of religious experience. As we shall see, philosophers in recent decades have thought that, in general, reflection on language is the most effective way to understand all forms of experience. But concern with language in religious matters is not new in the twentieth century. The early Christian church had very serious questions to answer as it clarified its doctrines and formulated its creeds. In this work linguistic considerations were unavoidable. In more recent centuries, the interpretation of scriptures has necessarily given rise to linguistic considerations. And comparable occupation with language is found among many of the other religions of the world.

Besides the language used in the expression of doctrine and creeds and in the writing of scripture, there is also the language used by religious people in performing certain specifically religious acts. It is established among them, for example, that unless certain very specific things are said in the performance of religious rites, the proper end of the rites will not have been achieved. In the celebration of the holy eucharist the priest must, in addition to making certain specified gestures, also be saying certain specified utterances. And when the people speak during such a rite, what they are saying cannot be properly understood unless it is taken as a prescribed element contributing to the whole of the rite which, in turn, must be understood within the framework of the whole religion. The general confession, for example, is more than a group of people saying they are sorry for their misdoings.

But, while these linguistic aspects of religion have always existed, our looking at them in just this way is a decidedly modern phenomenon. Its origin in large part is in the intensification during the twentieth century of philosophical interest in language as it is used in all forms of human life. Because of this interest philosophers have brought these life forms in for examination by looking at the language used by persons participating in them. This has included, besides religion, such forms as science, morality, politics, art, and philosophy itself. Some philosophers have been more generous than others in what they have said about the significance of language as it is employed by each.

So the proper historical locus for the study of this important body of literature on religious language is our own philosophical present. This is the period when the success of sciences has come through to make philosophers at last face up to their lurking doubts about the problems they have so long sought to solve and the methods they have employed in doing so. Scientists have provided us with positive knowledge of the world. They have done this by confining their investigations to what can be tested in experience. But philosophers have claimed to deal with much more than that. It is inevitable that they should have tried to convert the methods of the scientists to their own purposes, and that, having tried to confine their attention to the realm of experience, they should have ruled as outside the limits of knowledge all of that traditionally known as "transcendent." And since a great deal of what religion seems to be about is this "transcendent reality," the work of philosophers which followed this conversion was inevitably hostile toward religion.

Philosophers did not see their task as one of simply doing what scientists do. Rather, philosophers thought they saw even more clearly than they had in the past that they could not claim to deal with knowledge of the world. It seemed clear that the business of gathering knowledge was the scientists'. What could philosophers do? They could examine the concepts used by people whose business it was to gather knowledge. In this way they could avoid the occupations with a transcendent reality and confine their attention to obviously legitimate subjects without doing more or less badly the work which the scientists did well. They could confine their attention to understanding just what it was that made the difference between the scientist's successful description of the world and the empty babble of all the others, including the philosophers and the religious. So they asked the question, What is meaningful discourse?

This effect of science on philosophy has been working for over a century and has influenced the many philosophical movements we now label as "scientism." They admire the sciences and want to extend scientific methods to all other disciplines because, they contend, only these methods provide real knowledge. Any discipline which cannot employ these methods is obviously no discipline at all. The epitome of scientism is read in the twentieth-century philosophical movement known as Logical Positivism. It was a group of scientists, mathematicians, and philosophers formed soon after World War I and led by Moritz Schlick. It is they who brought philosophy to its present concern with language.

The Logical Positivists sought, in the name of "scientific philosophy," to free us from everything they regarded as nonsense. Their program was presented for the first time in English in the small but influential book by A. J. Ayer entitled *Language, Truth, and Logic*. This book gained for itself a great notoriety. It was particularly influential among religious thinkers, many of whom regarded it as a menace. Other religious thinkers seem to have had this book or its doctrines in mind when trying to find formulations of religion which might still appeal to modern minds.

The central doctrine of the book is the "Principle of Verifiability." In its classical form it reads "The meaning of a proposition is its method of verification." The idea is that the meaning of a sentence is exhausted by all of those sentences expressing what we could experience if the sentence in question is true. For example, let us consider the sentence "The guru is meditating." There are certain observations which would show this is true. One would be expressed by the sentence "Guru is very still." Another would be "Guru is kneeling with his eyes shut." Still another would be "Guru is pronouncing the meditation sound." The meaning of the sentence about the guru is the same as these and all other sentences which express observations we could make if the main sentence were true.

By contrast, sentences for which we can find no observation sentences will be properly designated as nonsense. It should be fairly obvious what significance this has for many if not all religious sentences. Ayer spells it out in such remarks as ". . . our view [is] that all utterances about the nature of God are nonsensical" and ". . . the religious utterances of the theist are not genuine propositions at all. . . ." [14] I leave as an exercise for the reader the development of a list of observation statements for the sentence "God cares for us."

Ironically, it became obvious after a while, if not to the most zealous, at least to the most intelligent Logical Positivists that exceedingly few sentences could meet their test of meaningfulness. All generalizations, for example, from the simplest such as "All men are mortal" to the more advanced such as Newton's inverse square law, could never have their meaning exhausted in sentences directly observable. The list of sentences would have to be infinite and so the verifications could never be complete. The response to this recognition was to loosen the requirement and say that a meaningful sentence has to be confirmable, that is, it need only have consequences which are verifiable. Thus the sentence is somehow indirectly verifiable even though all of the tests could not in practice be performed. This weakening of the verifiability principle was enough to make clear that the test for sense was not to be found in verifiability. Philosophers now wonder at the influence this principle had.

Religious thinkers express no regret at the passing of this period in the recent history of philosophy. One might almost detect a certain note of relief. But it is important to realize that, despite its inadequacy as a principle of meaning, the verifiability principle has shown something which cannot be ignored. The principle has failed as a universal touchstone for sense against nonsense, but it has taught us to ask what kind of evidence would establish or refute a certain claim, or what reason do we have for accepting it. In doing this we have discovered that besides scientifically verifiable ones there are many kinds of sentences and many of these are perfectly legitimate.[15]

Unfortunately, this in no way spells immediate legitimacy for religious sentences. For, acknowledging that there are many perfectly meaningful sentences which are not directly verifiable, one still has to ask—of at least certain religious sentences—just what sort they are. And a goodly number of them seem to be of just the sort which would call for verification and yet not seem to be verifiable at all. We have, in short, to apply to them that very pressure urged by the Logical Positivists.

One way this has been done is by noting that religious sentences, certain ones which seem to assert something factual, also seem to be held as true no matter what the facts are.[16] They seem not to be falsifiable. Such utterances as "God created the world," or "God loves us as a father loves his children" very much resemble assertions about the way things are. Yet religious people go on saying them, even when they have to admit that things are not the way these assertions, if true, would lead us to expect them to be.

Religious thinkers have responded in a number of ways. Some have offered interpretations of all religious assertions as being translatable into commands. For example, saying that God loves us is, according to this view, really just a way of saying the command that we love one another. Others have offered interpretations of religious assertions as being translatable into expressions of wishes. For example, saying that He shall come again in glory is, according to this view, really just a way of expressing the wish for a day when all wrongs will be righted and all evils dispersed, even though in saying this we do not exactly expect this to happen; or on a special day, certainly. Others might interpret such an utterance as less like a wish and more like the expression of one's feelings about present evils.

I mention, finally, still others who have offered interpretations of religious assertions as translatable into ethical assertions. Thus, like those who offer analyses of the first sort mentioned above, these thinkers would interpret "God is our father" as a concentrated expression of several ethical principles following from its implication that we are all siblings. Foremost among these would be the ethical principle that we ought to love one another and behave toward one another accordingly.

These are by no means all of the kinds of interpretation offered to empty religious utterances of their assertive character. But common to all of these and all others like them are two basic failures. First, they all succeed fairly well with a certain limited range of religious utterances and look good as long as attention is confined only to those. They fail to do justice to the wide range of religious utterances. For example, the ethical analysis works fairly well on "God is our father," less well on "God created the world," and not at all on "Jesus arose from the dead." To be sure, if any of these assertions is true, many things follow about how we should conduct ourselves, but this is different from saying the utterances are themselves merely ethical in content.

This brings us to the second failure of such analyses: they do not do justice to what religious people themselves think they are saying when they utter what we are here calling religious assertions. It is, I think, fair to say that most religious people think they are saying what the utterances would indicate they are saying. For example, if a religious person says, "Jesus is the son of God," he is saying something about the relationship between Jesus and God—two very special beings in a very special relationship, to be sure—but he is not saying anything, directly anyway, about ethics.

These considerations make the falsification issue more insistent. If attempts to remove the appearance of assertion will not do, then how can religious utterances really assert anything and still be compatible with any and every state of affairs? For to assert that something is the case is perforce to deny its negation. And whatever would count against the assertion in question is part of the meaning of its negation. Now knowing the meaning of an assertion's negation is for all practical purposes the same as knowing the meaning of that assertion. And this means that if there is nothing which counts against the alleged assertion, then there is nothing which it denies. This can be only if it never really asserted anything.

It seems to be the peculiar danger for religious utterances that, instead of their being rejected in the face of certain states of affairs apparently inconsistent with them, one so interprets their meaning that no inconsistency arises. And one keeps doing that, time and again, until there is little, if anything, left of the original assertion. The statements telling of the Second Coming are good examples. At one time the Second Coming was regarded as imminent. But as time passed these statements were qualified until today there are many who regard them as metaphorical or something else if they pay any attention to them at all. Thus, according to Anthony Flew, they die the death of a thousand qualifications.[17]

Notice that this is not to object to religious utterances because they are not verifiable. Rather, it is to object that they are not falsifiable. There seems to be nothing which *would* count against them, not that there is nothing which would count for them. They could be true in which case we could not expect to find anything counting against them—not decisively, anyway. But the point is that there seems to be nothing which even *could* count against certain religious utterances, and this makes one wonder whether they say anything at all.

A strategy employed by R. M. Hare in behalf of religious utterances is to admit that they are not assertions but at the same time to deny that they are either vacuous or entirely different from assertions.[18] Consider a college administrator with a psychological malady bordering on what we might call mild paranoia. The person believes that all students are subversives who desire to kill him as part of their plot to overthrow the American educational system. No matter how many of the most docile students we bring into his office to express their best wishes to him, he merely replies that it is part of the plot to put him off his guard. It is clear this person is deluded. Nothing is allowed to count against his belief, and so, according to Flew, there is no assertion. But that does not mean the person will not act and speak differently from a person not so deluded.

Whatever it is that makes this difference Hare calls a "blik." The college administrator has an insane blik, but we who are sane have a sane blik, not no blik. Thus there are right and wrong bliks. A blik is not any one or set of assertions, but which ones we have and of what kind they are make an important difference in our lives. And this is why it is important to have the right bliks. Think of our natural response to bridges—that they will not collapse when we drive over them—and then of someone who will not trust them. We can expand this thought experiment to one who will not trust roads, cars, or chairs, or anything at all until he gathers himself up into a ball in the corner. Now think of the lines in the Psalms: "The earth is weak and all of the inhabiters thereof: I bear up the pillars of it."

These religious words, Hare continues, are not the articulation of an explanation of the world order or just so many assertions about it. But without some blik or other there can be no explanation because we decide by our bliks what will count as an explanation. Say, for example, we believed that everything happens by pure chance. There is no assertion involved because what we believe is compatible with anything's happening or not happening. So nothing could count against it. Yet we would not explain, predict, or plan anything. This would make us very different from people who have the usual belief about the world order, even though we assert nothing different from them. This kind of difference exists between those who really believe in God and those who really do not.

Hare stresses the word "really" here. In the present era there are people who say they have no religious beliefs at all, but they have had a Christian upbringing and so continue to have the traditional Christian bliks. There are still enough such people so that it is difficult to know what it is really not to be a believing Christian and to know what difference the belief makes. And it is easy for people to say they are not religious because they do not really know what it is like to be without these bliks. More generally, we can appreciate the importance of bliks when we consider the many different kinds of bliks people may, in dropping the Christian ones, adopt in the coming age.

Another strategy is employed by Basil Mitchell.[19] His is to say that facts do count against religious utterances which thus are assertions according to Flew's test. For example, the fact of human suffering does count against the religious assertion that God loves humans. But, Mitchell adds, the religious person will not allow this or any fact to count decisively against it because he is committed to it by faith or, as we say, trust, in God. Thus religious persons are *like* those who one night meet a stranger, and on the basis of what he tells them are convinced that he is for them and to be trusted no matter what. Sometimes the stranger moves in mysterious ways, even against them, and this counts against their assertion "The stranger is for us." But they trust the stranger and it is just this mysterious movement which tries their faith.

After many such moves against them, they can conclude either that the stranger is not for them or that he is but has his reasons for acting against them. They will not, because of their faith in him, take the first alternative. How long can they hold to the second? This depends on the original impression the stranger made and whether they can continue to assign any sense at all to the assertion "He is for us." To apply this to religious assertions, saying "God loves us" in the face of human suffering, cannot just mean "humans suffer," but the difficulty is in saying just what it does mean in terms of what we can expect from God.

Nevertheless, Mitchell concludes that "God loves men" is like "The stranger is for us." It is not conclusively falsifiable. The committed Christian cannot take it any other way, but he has to avoid making it into a vacuous expression of reassurance making no difference to life. Mitchell believes he can avoid this and if he does not, he falters in faith as well as in logic.

Flew objects to Hare's analysis of Christian religious utterances as expressions of a blik rather than as assertions about the cosmos. As important as Hare's invention of the blik is for philosophy, its use in this case is misguided. So interpreted, religious utterances would be entirely unorthodox because they would involve no personal creator or Christian God. And so interpreted, religious utterances would become entirely fatuous because they would look like reasons and explanations but in fact neither be nor presuppose any assertions whatever.

Flew objects to Mitchell's parable of the stranger because there is an important difference between the stranger and God. The believers can easily excuse the ambiguous behavior of the stranger because he is a man. He may want to help but not be able. They cannot, however, say of the omnipotent and omniscient God that he would like to help but is not able. Mitchell is right in saying that the believer looks for an explanation which will make his beliefs square with the facts, but it is obvious from this instance that in the end he will have to resort to qualifications of his statement that "God cares for men." And, once started, his utterance is well on the way to that death of a thousand qualifications.

I. M. Crombie continues the debate in a way especially interesting to those analyzing religious language for the first time. For the sake of presentation, Crombie focuses on statements about God. He notes that they consist of two parts—that which is said and that which it is said about. The ordinary grammatical terms for these parts are "predicate" and "subject." In statements about God there is the subject term "God" used exclusively for such statements and this is its ordinary use. There is also a range of predicates borrowed from other contexts and their use in these statements is an extraordinary use.

Religious belief is built upon what individuals take to be signs of divine activity. This means that religious belief involves taking something as revelatory of God. Thus it involves an element of authority. A Christian's statements about God rest on the authority of Christ, and this is the essential clue to their logic. Crombie likens their function to that of parable, but he has his own special sense of "parable" which he illustrates by making reference to

Christ's action on Palm Sunday when he rode into Jerusalem on an ass.

According to Crombie, Christ's action was an act of teaching. First, it was written that Jerusalem's King would come in this manner. Crombie says, "Whoever, therefore, deliberately chose this method of entry, was saying in effect: 'What you are about to witness (namely my Passion, Death and Resurrection) is the coming of the Messianic King to claim his kingdom.'" Second, this shows something about how the prophecy of Messiah's kingdom is to be construed, that is, not in the ordinary sense, but in the sense of the royal kingship of the Crucified. Crombie goes on, "To interpret in this way is to teach by violent paradox, indeed, but nonetheless it is to teach. Part of the lesson is that it is only the kings of the Gentiles that lord it over their subjects; if any man will be a king in Israel (God's chosen people), he must humble himself as a servant; part of it is that the crucifixion is to be seen as Messianic, that is as God's salvation of His chosen people." [20]

Crombie then lays out the logical structure of this encounter with the story. To take the story at its face value is to get it all wrong. To take the story in the light of all that is revealed in the Law and the Prophets about God's purposes for his people is to come much closer to the correct interpretation. Then Christ's suffering is appropriate, something about God's purposes for man is revealed, and from this something about God can be inferred. Isaiah's teaching about humility and sacrifice will illuminate Christ's entry as forecasting that God's purposes will be accomplished by a man who in humble obedience fulfills the Law and the Prophets. But the interpretation of the parable will never be fully transparent.

Crombie brings his view to the verification question in this way:

Must we, to preserve our claim to be making assertions, be

prepared to say what would count against them? Let us see how far we can do so. Does anything count against the assertion that God is merciful? Yes, suffering. Does anything count decisively against it? No, we reply, because it is true. Could anything count decisively against it? Yes, suffering which was utterly, eternally, and irredeemably pointless. Can we then design a crucial experiment? No, because we can never see all of the picture. Two things at least are hidden from us; what goes on in the recesses of the personality of the sufferer, and what shall happen hereafter.

Well, then, the statement that God is merciful is not testable; it is compatible with any and every tract of experience which we are in fact capable of witnessing. It cannot be verified; does this matter? [21]

Crombie sees the demand for verifiability as legitimate, but also as the conflation of two demands. The first is that a factual statement cannot be such that verification is irrelevant to it. In other words, it cannot be such that a person trying to verify it would *eo ipso* not have understood it. This would be the case with a person who tried to verify the statement "Killing is wrong" by observing human behavior. But there are factual statements which cannot be verified even though it is not exactly because of logical considerations. An example is "Caesar had mutton before he crossed the Rubicon." The second is that I must know what it would be to test the statement in question if I am to be said to understand the statement. This demand has to do, not with the logical character of the statement, but with the communication value it has for me. One must be reasonably clear about how the situation of which the statement in question is true would differ from a situation of which the statement is false.

There is nothing about religious utterances which logically precludes testing them. For example, suffering counts as evidence against the statement "God is loving." But the Christian holds that this is only *prima facie* evidence. This much evidence will not determine the truth status of the statement, but this does not mean that the statement does not meet the first demand outlined above. There is no logical mistake in discussing the evidence. It is just that our experience is so limited that we cannot settle the matter once and for all.

There is also nothing about religious utterances which makes it impossible for me to know what it would be like to test any one of them. In terms of parable, "God loves us" is very similar to "Father loves us." Sometimes father is strict with us and sometimes he punishes us, but this does not mean that it is impossible for us to know when father might lose control and not love us anymore. As we have already seen, we cannot in fact test "God loves us," but the statement still communicates because it is a statement with an ordinary predication despite its extraordinary subject. Certainly, we do not know how and to what the parable applies, but within the parable we know what is meant. And we believe the parable does apply to something—how and to what we may hope sometime to discover.

In sum, then, this is to reject Flew's claim that religious statements are vacuous because they are not verifiable. Crombie tries to explain how it is that religious utterances do communicate and are properly understood as factual and in some sense verifiable even though we cannot now verify them.

If we take into account the logic of religious belief Crombie presents and the idea that verification will come in the indefinite future when we are able to see the parts of the whole picture of reality (which when put into place will show us the design of the whole), then we cannot avoid thinking back to the discussion of natural religion in Chapter I. Most of the objections presented there against natural religion have force against Crombie's discussion of religious language. If one can once get past the difficulty of making a sense of the divine and relating it to the world on the basis of experience, then most of the difficulties raised by the challenge of verification disappear. As in Chapter I this did not appear to be likely.

Further, Crombie's response to the challenge of verification is in effect to ask us to wait forever if necessary for our verification. This response would appear to deserve the treatment given to any hypothesis which is built upon the mere possibility that it holds water.

Finally, we can see from Crombie's discussion of religious language and the objections which apply to it that the linguistic turn of the problems of philosophy of religion and the seemingly new challenge of the principle of verifiability do not really bring very much new to philosophy of religion. This is probably more Flew's fault than Crombie's. In any case, the fundamental problem for religion from the standpoint of philosophy is to be able to maintain the existence of something, no matter what, which can require the special response to the world and life called for by the particular religions.

# V

## Religion
## and the Modern World

*The Meaning of Life.*

In the preceding chapters we have seen time and again how the problems in the philosophy of religion revolve about the notion of faith. In the previous chapter we saw how religious experience cannot be understood apart from it. And in earlier chapters we have seen how even the most fundamental concepts of religion depend on it. The religious person will insist that without his commitments he cannot achieve full and proper understanding of life and the world. We have, in short, seen the importance of faith in understanding. This is the meaning of *"credo ut intelligam,"* I believe that I might understand.

The historical direction of these chapters might possibly suggest that gradually there has been less and less room for that primary belief. It might even appear that today it is appropriate to say "I understand and so I cannot believe." Whether that is suggested in the preceding chapters or not, there have been many modern writers who have suggested it. Too much understanding is the enemy of belief and commitment. Dostoevsky suggests this in the person of the Underground Man:

What stone wall? Why, the laws of nature, of course; the conclusions of the natural sciences, of mathematics. When they are through proving to you that you descend from the monkey, it will do you no good to screw up your nose—you'll just have to take it. Trust them to prove to you that a single drop of your own fat is bound to be dearer to you, when you come down to it, than a hundred thousand human lives and that this conclusion is an answer to all this talk about virtue and duty, and other ravings and superstitions. So you can take it for what it is—there's nothing else you can do; it's like two and two make four. That's arithmetic. Just try and disprove it!

"Wait a minute," they'll call out to you, "why protest? Two and two do make four. Nature doesn't ask your advice. She isn't interested in your preferences or whether or not you approve of her laws. You must accept nature as she is with all the consequences that that implies. So a wall is a wall, etc., etc. . . ." [1]

And yet, ironically, this wall could not have been built without a very special set of beliefs about God. As Alfred North Whitehead writes,

But for science something more is wanted than a general sense of the order in things. . . . I mean the inexpugnable belief that every detailed occurrence can be correlated with its antecedents in a perfectly definite manner, exemplifying general principles. Without this belief the incredible labours of scientists would be without hope. . . . How has this conviction been so vividly implanted on the European mind?

When we compare this tone of thought in Europe with the attitude of other civilizations when left to themselves, there seems but one source for its origin. It must come from the medieval insistence on the rationality of God, conceived as with the personal energy of Jehovah and with the rationality of a Greek philosopher. Every detail was supervised and ordered: the search into nature could only result in the vindication of the faith in rationality. Remember that I am not talking of the explicit beliefs of a few individuals. What I mean is the impress on the European mind arising from the unquestioned faith of centuries. . . . My explanation is that the faith in the possibility of science, generated antecedently to the development of modern scientific theory, is an unconscious derivative from medieval theology. [2]

These two quoted passages dramatize the drift of modern thought away from the personal relation between God and man. They suggest a meaning for the words of Nietzsche's Zarathustra, who pronounced "God is dead." Unfortunately, that meaning is ambiguous, allowing both the idea that there is no longer a God-guaranteed place for the person in the universe, and the idea that there is no longer a God-guaranteed unity of truth for scientists to pursue. In this section we cannot hope to do more than trace out this ambiguity along one general theme. That theme is the quest for the meaning of life in the modern world.

The suggestion, then, is that, while modern thought may have had its origin in belief in God, ideas have developed in such a way that belief in God has become impossible, and so has faith in a world order in which the individual is significant. The growth of science, for one thing, has left us with an understanding of the world in terms of itself rather than in terms with outside reference —an understanding in which the world is "just there," neither the result nor object of any intelligent purpose.

A common response to this way of understanding the world is that it renders life meaningless. It leaves no room for the typical religious answer to the question "What is the meaning of life?" We must not leave the question here. It may well be that the traditional religious answer will no longer do, but this does not mean that we must conclude that life is meaningless. We need first to understand the meaning of the question "What is the meaning of life?" What is it that one wants when he utters it? Is it a meaningful question at all?

As I suggested a moment ago, there is reason to believe that the question depends upon religious thinking and may not be meaningful apart from belief in God or some other "outside" reference.

We can explore this idea further in the context of an interesting lecture entitled "The Meaning of Life" [3] given by an analytical philosopher, Kurt Baier. Baier begins his lecture with a quotation from Leo Tolstoy, who at fifty and the height of his literary powers became obsessed by the fear that life had no meaning. Thus Tolstoy wrote:

> At first I experienced moments of perplexity and arrest of life, as though I did not know what to do or how to live; and I felt lost and became dejected. But this passed, and I went on living as before. Then these moments of perplexity began to recur oftener and oftener, and always in the same form. They were always expressed by the questions: What is it for? What does it lead to? At first it seemed to me that these were aimless and irrelevant questions. I thought that it was all well known, and that if I should ever wish to deal with the solution it would not cost me much effort; just at present I had not time for it, but when I wanted to, I should be able to find the answer. The questions however began to repeat themselves frequently, and to demand replies more and more insistently; and like drops of ink always on one place they ran together into one black blot.[4]

Before going on with Baier's remarks, I want to quote further from Tolstoy for the sake of emphasis. In the next paragraph, Tolstoy goes on:

> Then occurred what happens to everyone sickening with a mortal internal disease. At first trivial signs of indisposition appear to which the sick man pays no attention; then these signs reappear more and more often and merge into one uninterrupted period of suffering. The suffering increases and, before the sick man can look round, what he took for a mere indisposition has already become more important to him than anything else in the world—it is death!
>
> That was what happened to me. I understood that it was no casual indisposition but something very important, and that if these questions constantly repeated themselves they would have to be answered. And I tried to answer them. The questions seemed such stupid, simple, childish ones; but as soon as I touched them and tried to solve them I at once became convinced, first, that they are not childish and stupid but the most important and profound of life's questions; and secondly that, try as I would, I could not solve them.[5]

This perplexity expressed by Tolstoy in the nineteenth century did not exist, according to Baier, for the medieval Christian. For the latter the world was created by God; and man, the crown of creation, was created in the image of God, placed in the Garden of Eden on Earth which was at the center of the universe created for man's enjoyment; and, though man fell from grace, he was redeemed by God through Jesus Christ.

While to the medieval Christian the meaning of his life was clear and everything, despite appearances, was for the best and to be accepted, to the modern man things are quite different. There is no playwright God and no life drama in which man works out his salvation for something greater than he knows. The world is understood or understandable and man even has considerable control over it. There is no need to accept mysteries and there is no need to accept what happens to him. Man can change his condition. Science is in principle able to give complete and real explanation of everything in the universe.

Thus, it is not correct to think as do some thinkers, most notably certain existentialists, that acceptance of the scientific world picture is one's reason for believing that the universe is unintelligible and therefore meaningless. It may be true that after having been taught the Christian world view one may, discovering the power of scientific explanation, be so affected that he says life is meaningless. But such a person cannot say it is scientific understanding which has made the world meaningless. Sometimes it is said that scientific explanations are only provisional and incomplete and so require supplementation by religious explanation. But, in light of the preceding point, this would be asking for supplementation for a method from a source which that method has already displaced.

Indeed, it seems that the more we understand scientifically, the more it becomes clear that human life has no purpose. From astronomy we learn the earth was not created but rather evolved from hot nebulae, whirling aimlessly through space, which cooled, forming the solar system. Life appeared on earth because circumstances were propitious, but they will not remain so forever. From biology we learn that man too evolved and resembles, more than anything else, the naked ape. We can understand man's situation very well from this point of view. His life is a struggle for survival and with a few brief snatches of joy amid disease, famine, and war, it ends in death. Nothing like purpose or meaning appears in this view. This does not make life unintelligible: it only shows life to be without *purpose*.

But before we conclude that life is meaningless, we must look at the meaning of the word "purpose." We may distinguish two senses of this word. In its first and basic sense it means purpose as attributed to human beings. It serves in answers to the question, "Why did you do that?" In its second sense it means purpose as normally attributed to things. In this second sense it serves in answers to the question, "What is it for?" The first sense involves an evaluation. A life without any seriousness of purpose is insignificant. But, Baier claims, this sense of purpose is not ruled out by a scientific understanding of life. There are still important undertakings for man. We should note here, however, that we have a right to ask Baier how he decides what is important if life has no purpose in the medieval Christian sense.

In Baier's second sense of "purpose" no evaluation is involved. If something has a purpose, for example, a row of trees, then it has and that is that. If it does not, there is nothing in any evaluative sense *wrong* with this. But in this sense, which seems to be like the traditional religious sense of purpose, it would be wrong for man to have a purpose. For this would imply that man is some kind of means, as it would were we to ask a man in livery, "What are you for?" It is thus degrading to have a purpose in this sense. It is this sense which Baier takes to be the sense of the medieval world picture. Baier regards this as the bad thing about the Christian view of man. It gives man a purpose by degrading him. Man is God's Frankenstein with orders from God.

Lacking purpose in this sense does not mean our lives are destined to be aimless or insignificant. Of course, there are some people who have a need to be for something, if nothing more than as a servant. The scientific view of man does disturb them. But it is only because life cannot have the same purpose they *thought* it had, not that their individual lives can have no purpose.

There is another aspect of the traditional religious idea of purpose and that is the notion of God's plan in which each individual as a part of the plan is *assured* of significance whatever it might be. To be able to assess this properly, we must notice the difference between a life's being worthwhile and its being part of a transcending purpose. Now in the former case we know what this is. An example would be dedicating one's life to cancer research. In the latter case we know what is usually meant, i.e., a person's participating in God's plan; but we do not know what that plan is. Because of the problem of evil, we cannot formulate God's plan.

Moreover, Christianity requires that we exalt that which is wholly other than man and that we abase the individual to the limit. Christianity is inconsistent with the presupposition of morality—that man is not wholly dependent on something other, that man has free will and is in principle capable of responsibility. The Christian ideas of grace and original sin are obviously incompatible with this presupposition. Thus, according to Baier, we have our choice between insisting upon some overall purpose in which we are but creatures, and denying any overall purpose thus gaining significance as human beings.

One might object to Baier's reasoning so far by saying that the real question is whether any individual human life can in any way have meaning if it ends in death.

There seems to be nothing in this life which can transcend death. Baier responds to this by treating it as a natural objection from someone who has been taught the traditional Christian view that life is not in itself worth living but that we are forbidden to end it because it belongs to God. So the real question is whether this is the proper evaluation of life.

According to Baier the medieval Christian view and the modern Christian view, to the extent it resembles the medieval, are fundamentally misguided. They are misguided in the way they make their evaluation of this life. We normally make evaluations using criteria which are relevant to whatever we are evaluating. The criteria used in evaluating bulls are different from those used in evaluating bathing beauties. There is implicit in each case an average which serves as the norm, and we see how each entry meets or surpasses it.

It is likewise in the evaluation of life. We take the average as the norm. But Christianity takes the perfect life as the norm, sees that we cannot have it, and then concludes that life on earth is not worthwhile—only heaven is. This is as misguided as refusing to call something tall unless it is infinitely tall. And, as for death, Baier says, it is irrelevant. If life can be worthwhile and there is every reason to think so, then it can be worthwhile even though it is short. So life has no meaning beyond itself, but this does not entail that individual lives can have no meaning in the sense of being worthwhile.

We have in Baier an attempt to formulate an alternative to theism. He offers an answer to the question, "Why go on living?" not in general, but by saying that the life of the person asking may in fact be worthwhile. The belief that life cannot be worthwhile unless there is a future life rests on a misunderstanding of the nature of evaluations. Unfortunately, we should note here that Baier's argument, if sound, would not show that there are any worthwhile lives. It would only show that there may in fact be.

Whether there is anything anyone would want to live for still remains to be seen.

The doctrine that life here on earth is worthwhile for its own sake is commonly known as humanism. In its cruder formulations it takes mankind as the supreme being. According to the humanist August Comte (1798–1857), the founder of modern sociology, humanity is the greatest being. And he thought of all mankind as a kind of singular being. Only in humanity do we find a striving for the improvement of life and society. Because man is sacrosanct, altruistic acts are always good and a life devoted to undertaking them will always be worthwhile. We can notice here, though, the essential requirement that humanity be posited as the highest being and value. Without this, it would be less clear that any single life could be worthwhile. With it, an individual life can be worthwhile by deriving value from serving the supreme being, humanity.

Here we must ask just how valuable mankind is. The question is awkward, but only because it reflects upon this religious humanism. We may grant that man has broken with nature in the sense that he can control it and he can even modify himself. It is this ability that has suggested to some humanists that man can progress. But, despite these considerations, we can still ask what man's place in the universe is, and whether it is in any sense important. It is true that he can control some of nature, but we still wonder how this makes man more valuable than anything else, or valuable at all. And, supposing man is important in some sense on earth, we might well wonder what man's importance is in the entire universe or even our galaxy.

Man is capable of progress in the sense of making technical progress, but there is some question whether we should call this progress at all. In the first place, it is not exactly clear just what it means to make progress in this context. In the second place, it is exactly technical progress that dramatizes man's moral or spiritual incompetence in the present age. Perhaps there was a time when what man could do to nature was impressive. Now it is positively frightening. It is quite possible that many of the ways we have tried to do things to help fellow humans may in the long run have disastrous consequences, not only for the whole species, but for all life on this planet.

Implicit in the preceding remarks is the philosophical question, What is the source of value? Without any external source, it has to be something about man himself. Comte thought he had to posit the absolute worth of mankind in order to make the species the source. But when we test this move, it seems to come down to the idea that mankind is important because men are interested in what they and other men do. This is not really to say that mankind is important at all. Rather, it is to say that what men do is important to them. This seems to be what Baier has in mind. What men do and judge worthwhile will be decided by men on the basis of what interests them. On this way of thinking all grandiose notions such as "the meaning of life" and "the progress of mankind" may be disposed of with no loss. A life is judged worthwhile when the person living it has done worthwhile things or had worthwhile experiences, and this is decided in purely human terms.

The theist would object to this as shortsighted. For him Baier's position is nothing more than a refusal to look beyond immediate human occupations; and any position such as Baier's does not do justice to the human condition. Each life will end and with it everything it valued, and, knowing this now, the living will not be able to place value on anything, not even a human life. Granted that, while life goes on, certain things such as food and drink, love, and health will be important. But when the world grows cold again and all life has passed away, what will they be worth then? Indeed, human undertakings are important only because human life continues. But why should it go on at all?

If we now turn to the work of Albert Camus, especially

*The Myth of Sisyphus,* we can explore this question more fully. Camus tries to keep the human condition fully in mind, even the fact of the finality of death, and yet to give an answer to the question, "Why go on living?" Also, we shall be able to see how very religious or dependent upon religious thought Camus' notion of the absurd really is.

Camus appears to operate within a basically Judeo-Christian ambience of life problems. His problems are parasitical upon these religious ways of thinking in the sense that his problems are unintelligible and uninteresting apart from them.

Camus asks, What is the meaning of life? He rules out from the beginning answers referring to what he calls eternal values or verities. His answer must come through reasoning about both man's condition and his choices, if he really has any choices. This is the unjustified assumption that the correct description of man's condition excludes considerations of eternal values. Camus qualifies this exclusion by saying that eternal values do not seem to weigh with people today. But this is still curious because it implies that the correct description of the human condition is one which can gain popular assent. Specifically, Camus asks why should one go on living rather than commit suicide? An answer to this question, he thinks, may lead us to an answer as to the meaning of life.

Camus' fundamental notion is the *absurd.* To understand it we have first to see that we are living in a universe suddenly divested of illusions, where man now finds himself an alien, a stranger. This divorce between man and his life is the experience of the absurd. And there is a connection between this experience and suicide, i.e., the question of suicide. The exact relationship between suicide and the absurd is what Camus wants to explore and he wants to ask if suicide really is the solution to the absurd. If what a man believes must determine his action, belief in the absurdity of life must dictate certain conduct. Does the absurd dictate death?

Strictly speaking, the experience of the absurd is not the

notion of the absurd. The latter is not in man or in the world but in the two in confrontation. Camus explains it as follows:

> If I accuse an innocent man of a monstrous crime, if I tell a virtuous man that he has coveted his own sister, he will reply that this is absurd. His indignation has its comical aspect. But it also has its fundamental reason. The virtuous man illustrates by that reply the definitive antinomy existing between the deed I am attributing to him and his life-long principles. "It's absurd" means "It's impossible" but also "It's contradictory." If I see a man armed only with a sword attack a group of machine guns, I shall consider his act to be absurd. But it is so solely by virtue of the disproportion between his intention and the reality he will encounter, of the contradiction I notice between his true strength and the aim he has in view. . . . I am thus justified in saying that the feeling of absurdity does not spring from the mere scrutiny of a fact or an impression, but that it bursts from the comparison between a bare fact and a certain reality, between an action and the world that transcends it. The absurd is essentially a divorce. It lies in neither of the elements compared; it is born of their confrontation.[6]

Camus emphasizes that the absurd is not in man or the world but in the two together and these cannot be divided.

Camus marks an important difference between himself and existentialist philosophers. They all suggest escape from the absurd. They see the universe "closed" to anything but the human. This crushing fact they somehow turn into a reason for hope. This hope is religous. For example, Kierkegaard, with all due respect to the subtlety of his reasoning, takes the leap. That which led him to despair of the meaning of this life gives life its truth and clarity. Camus thinks this is philosophical suicide.

Camus wants to remain faithful to the experience of the absurd—to that "divorce between the mind that desires and the world that disappoints, my nostalgia for unity, this fragmented universe and the contradiction that binds them together."[7] Others suppress the absurd by denying one of its terms. The question is whether one can live with the absurd or whether he, as a person who would be at one with himself, must conclude that there is no reason to go on living.

Camus answers his question by rejecting any leap of faith and at the same time by rejecting suicide. His reasons for rejecting the leap of faith are already clear: this would really be avoiding the absurd. But it is equally clear that suicide would be avoiding the absurd too. For living an experience, being true to it, is accepting it fully. The only way to do this is to keep it before you.

Thus Camus began by asking if life had to have meaning to be lived and now he arrives at the conclusion that life will be lived better if it has no meaning. Living is keeping the absurd alive—above all, by contemplating it. This is neither suicide nor the leap of faith. It is what Camus calls revolt. This gives life its value. This, too, gives life a new freedom. For, completely turned toward death, man is released from all external pressures. The most important part of this is freedom from the humdrum of routine living. This means the end of living a good life and instead living most fully. But to go into this notion would take us into too many directions for adequate coverage here.

At the beginning of my remarks on Camus, I said that I thought his ambience is religious despite itself. Whether I can really make this claim stick is not so important as what exploring it a little further might show about religion and religious thinking. Putting Camus' starting point generally and perhaps somewhat crudely, the absurd comes about from man's realization of his alienation from the world. Things do not go at all the way man would have them go, and yet he lives with them. We might grant the clearly nonreligious aspect of this starting point: the absurd is because God is not. But absurd is only if man is different from the world. If he is not, then what alienation is becomes unclear.

Now man is different from the world only if he is viewed nonbiologically and nonpsychologically, namely, as a creature of God in the image of God. Of course, man, even as a psychobiological being, can feel the absurdities of life. He can feel them, experience them, in all of the forms Camus discusses. But, unless there is any reason to expect that the world was or might have been different in such a way as to accommodate man's intentions, talk of the absurd comes to little more than pointing up some of the ridiculous aspects of life. I would not say that this does not have its place. But this is far different from *realizing* the absurd; for, as Camus himself says, the feeling of the absurd is not *the absurd*.

A man may feel frustrated, confused, and he may even feel that things are fated in some sense not to go his way. But this is no more reason to call the world absurd than it is reason to try to find the meaning of life in relationships among events in which he finds himself. Thus, in the case of an airplane crash, one might speculate on the meaning of the plane's going down on Christmas day or he might search for a causal explanation. What would be absurd in the ordinary sense of the word would be for an atheist to go up to the scene of the crash and shake his fist at the sky. We might "understand" but we would very likely try to direct his thoughts elsewhere. What is absurd about this atheist is that he is behaving as if he were in a religious context where he might have expected something else but does not get it. There is no reason for man to expect life to be any different from what it is unless he is religious. What happens in life just happens, no matter how absurd it seems to us. So when Camus offers his answer and calls upon us to revolt, we must ask "Against what?" and "Why?"

This conclusion makes one wonder what lies behind Camus' starting point—that we cannot accept appeals to a transcendent reality. Is it modern man who cannot? And is it really impossible for modern man to believe in a world not covered by science? It would seem that Camus owes us an argument demonstrating that we cannot reasonably believe in an unseen world. Such belief may be out of fashion in modern culture, but that is not the same as its being logically unjustifiable. This takes us to the heart of the matter.

Camus has been important because his work sums up the increasing disillusionment with man's ability to progress ever onwards toward some future state of perfection. He has not shown that traditional religious beliefs are philosophically untenable. By contrast, the theistic view we have discussed most in this book, the Judeo-Christian view, has taken a skeptical view of man's capacities all along. It has always repudiated the confident optimism of modern civilization now in full bloom in our practically secular society. The Judeo-Christian view is that human life is essentially tragic and full of suffering. It rejects the belief that man's progress is inevitable and that his course is both right and just. Man's only hope for salvation is through divine intervention.

At the same time, the Judeo-Christian view of man repudiates pessimism too. To say there is no hope for the future of mankind is to blaspheme. Man can be saved. He is a creature of God and loved by God. If he is alone, it is only because he is in rebellious estrangement from God. In this state of alienation man feels the wrath of God. Camus wants to come to terms with this alienation, somehow to solve it. In the Judeo-Christian view this cannot be done, and to think of doing it is to misconstrue man's tragic situation by seeing it too closely.

These reflections do not, of course, resolve the differences between Camus and traditional theists and they do not establish the view of either as superior. But they do, I think, show the deep similarities between Camus' thought and typical religious thought. Moreover, they both stand on one side in contrast to Baier's view which tries to allow us room to say that a life is what you make it. They both try to provide an answer to those who have asked, who have despaired. Baier's view is for those who do not need an answer.

To be sure, Baier insists that there is no question. But I think there are people who have asked the question all the same, people who have found that human occupations cannot dispel the knowledge in a lonely hour that we exist for such a brief time. Again, this is not to say that a person cannot accept his inevitable death, but at another level where one contemplates nothingness such reconciliation seems impossible.

It is this contemplation of emptiness which is the starting point for the next alternative to theism I shall discuss.

### Zen Buddhism.

The problem of problems, as D. T. Suzuki puts it, is just this struggle between the finite and the infinite, man in his limitations against that which limits him.[8] Suzuki equates these elements with those in the struggle between the intellect and a higher power and even with the flesh and the spirit. This struggle awakens the religious consciousness and then all avenues of escaping or terminating it are sought. Like Tolstoy, those thus awakened seek the answer in books, lectures, sermons, and holy exercises.

Zen answers by appealing to facts of personal experience rather than to book knowledge—that known through looking into life rather than through using the intellect. The intellect makes us raise the question it cannot answer by itself, and so we must go beyond it to something more enlightening. By leading us to this and other questions, the intellect moves us out of blissful ignorance, but it cannot restore us to peace. Its power to make us aware of our ignorance makes us mistakenly consider it enlightening. But the perpetual coming and going of philosophical systems shows that it is not. And even if it were, we could not wait for it to churn out the ultimate solution to the problem of life. Zen does not rely on the intellect.

The idea is to eliminate anything intervening, particularly the words and letters of the intellect, between personal experience and reality. Thus, according to favorite Zen analogies,

> To point at the moon a finger is needed, but woe to those who take the finger for the moon; a basket is welcome to carry our fish home, but when the fish are safely on the table why should we eternally bother ourselves with the basket? [9]

Taking distinctions of the intellect such as that between the finite and the infinite too seriously is like taking the basket for the food, i.e., a fact of life. But when we are hungry we eat. Life as lived suffices. It is complete as is each one of us. The intellect has its place, but one cannot without interrupting life look into life through the intellect.

Zen has its own way of leading one out of the contradictory maze of the intellect toward one's own being. The end of this way is Buddhahood where all conflicts are harmonized. Zen does not give reasons or invoke general principles in explanations. It keeps to the real and in doing so it even seems to stand in the face of contradictions. Zen is a way of grasping reality in its unity. When one sees into his own nature, he sees there is no distinction between oneself and the world. He sees this in an intuition, an insight, which is called *satori*. Thus, of the two ways of dealing with nature—conceptually, i.e., through analysis and description, or contemplatively, i.e., through being at one with nature—Zen is the latter.

Zen masters have ways of dislodging their novices from the habits of thought so that they might be filled with enlightenment. If a novice keeps pressing for reasons or explanations, the master may respond with physical force—deliver a blow or eject him from the room—for the sake of bringing him enlightenment. Also, the master may just give a nonsense answer for the novice to puzzle out and, in failing to solve it, to see the futility of his questions. This is a *koan*. Here are two famous koans:

A monk asked Tung-shan, "Who is the Buddha?" and received the reply: "Three measures of flax."

The great Japanese monk Hakuin replied to a novice by clapping both hands and then asking, "What sound does one hand make?" [10]

A master may also give in answer a *mondo* which is a puzzling dialogue. Here is a mondo:

A monk who saw Yao-shan meditating asked: "In this motionless position what are you thinking?"
"Thinking that which is beyond thinking."
"How do you go about thinking that which is beyond thinking?"
"By an act of not-thinking." [11]

The point of these is to get the novice to realize that reason is misleading and that it must be given up before one reaches final enlightenment.

We can see in these the basic idea in Zen that we are somehow deceived through intellection into finding a struggle in the place where there is only peace and this is here with us now. Salvation must be found here in the finite. Beyond finite things there is no infinite. Seeking the transcendental only blinds us to this world and to ourselves. In turning within we can pass into the One. There we must be silent, but there we are restored to Unity.

Too much has been left out of this account of Zen Buddhism for general remarks to be appropriate, and probably they would not be appropriate under any circumstances. I want only to say that it is as different from any of the preceding alternatives to theism as it is from theism itself. It not only rejects the transcendental but it also does not deify man as humanism does, nor does it drop the question of the meaning of existence as Baier does, nor does it hold there is no answer to the question as Camus does. Then, again, it seems to deify man, to drop the question of meaning, and to hold there is no answer. This is not so puzzling given the Zen view of the intellect and of explanations. But we have to ask whether we can accept this view. A Zen master may be able to make us feel silly asking, but we can still wonder why he thinks he should.

### The Death of God and Radical Christianity.

This development in contemporary theology, whose fate is still quite uncertain, may be discussed to advantage after Zen Buddhism. It makes much of the uniqueness of Christianity and one way it does this is in contrast to the movement toward unity we saw in Zen and which is typical of Oriental religions. It also seeks to resolve the major difficulties of theism while preserving essential Christianity. Some assessment of whether and how it succeeds is important to our philosophical study of religion. This theology succeeds, if indeed it does, by propounding a religionless Christianity. Obviously, such a development cannot but interest the philosopher of religion.

Death-of-God theology is less a set of theological principles than the work of a cluster of theologians who during the sixties have discovered strong affinities, if not solidarity of opinion, in their theological responses to the growing and practically complete secularism of the modern world. As Thomas J. J. Altizer and William Hamilton, foremost among them, have explained, the phrase "death of God" might have as many as ten different meanings depending on who is using it.[12] And the meanings range from old-fashioned atheism to theistic skepticism about our ability to name God.

The death-of-God theologians have a common point of departure, however, in a letter written on April 30, 1944, by Dietrich Bonhoeffer while he was held in prison by the Nazis who on April 9, 1945, sent him to the gallows.

The thing that keeps coming back to me is, what *is* Christianity, and indeed what *is* Christ, for us to-day? The time when men could be told everything by means of words, whether theological or simply pious, is over, and so is the time of inwardness and conscience, which is to say the time of religion as such. We are proceeding towards a time of no religion at all: men as they are now simply cannot be religious any more. Even those who honestly describe themselves as "religious" do not in the least act up to it, and so when they say "religious" they evidently mean something quite different. Our whole nineteen-hundred-year-old Christian preaching and theology rests upon the "religious premise" of man. What we call Christianity has always been a pattern—perhaps a true pattern—of religion. But if one day it becomes apparent that this *a priori* "premise" simply does not exist, but was an historical and temporary form of human self-expression, i.e. if we reach the stage of being radically without religion—and I think this is more or less the case already, else how is it, for instance, that this war, unlike any of those before it, is not calling forth any "religious" reaction?—what does that mean for "Christianity"? [13]

Death-of-God theologians believe this day has come. Christian theology is now in what is probably the most serious crisis since its beginning.

This crisis appears in three places. First, it has become increasingly difficult to base theology on the Bible. Greater historical and scholarly understanding of the Bible, especially the New Testament, indicates we cannot have objective knowledge of the historical Jesus—the very anchor of Christian faith. What modern scholarship has been able to discover is a Jesus who, in Albert Schweitzer's words, is a "stranger and enigma to our time." [14] Jesus appears as a deluded Jewish fanatic whose ministry and teaching presupposed the end of the world was at hand. This is totally irrelevant to our time and situation.

Second, theology which speaks of the traditional theistic God of the West can no longer be heard by contemporary man. For him, God is dead. Although Kierkegaard was the first modern theologian who identified authentic human existence with the God-relation, which is completely subjective, this subjectivity was still Christian. This is no longer true, and one cannot identify the existential with existence in faith. Thus Kierkegaard understood how profoundly pagan the new reality of modern man was. "Objective" knowledge of modern philosophy was not religiously neutral, but, on the contrary, the negation of faith. But contemporary theologians have not the recourse Kierkegaard had.

Third, the collapse of Christendom has led to a crisis in the relation of the community of faith to social, political, and economic institutions. In the post-Christian West, these institutions are constituted and operated without reference to Christianity. Important decisions are made setting us on a course past Christianity. Modern theology, by setting faith against the secular world, has placed faith where it is gradually being forgotten.

Altizer's theology, which I shall single out as it is the most boldly radical, is a response to these three areas of theological crisis. It takes its direction, allegedly, from Friedrich Nietzsche who, according to Martin Heidegger, ended the metaphysical tradition of the West in proclaiming "God is dead." So ends the idea of transcendence, and so ends the metaphysical hierarchy from which existing beings can derive their meaning. This is exactly how Baier sees the situation. But Altizer believes further that the death of God or, more deeply, the willing of the death of God, is dialectical. We must view it in terms of what it makes possible for us.

For Nietzsche, a No-saying to God, i.e., to transcendence, allows a Yes-saying to human existence, i.e., to the here and now, or what Altizer calls the post-Christian existential "now." Thus, Altizer thinks, absolute transcendence is transformed into absolute immanence, and all powers once bestowed upon the Beyond come to Being here and now. This, Altizer thinks, is the meaning of Nietzsche's vision of Eternal Recurrence—the view that there is neither creation nor purpose as Christianity teaches, but only the endless repetition of each moment, each now, in immense time cycles.

Eternal Recurrence is thus the antithesis of the Christian God. But, even though Nietzsche rejected God and Christ, these were figures of Christianity, and so his attack upon them is less likely a rejection of Jesus than a rejection of religion. Nietzsche's Zarathustra could even be a modern dialectical image of the non-Christian Jesus. Thus, to trace the dialectic, we see first the death of objective Christianity in Kierkegaard's faith as radical subjectivity and we see next the death of Kierkegaard's subjectivity in the radically profane Now of Eternal Recurrence. In other words, the New Creation of Zarathustra, Eternal Recurrence, is a dialectical descendant of the New Creation of Jesus, the Kingdom of God.

To be sure, to get a thorough understanding of Altizer's thought here the reader must know something of Nietzsche's work and he must know something about what Altizer means by "dialectical." For the former I have space here only to refer the reader to Nietzsche's work. For the latter I can add that one can only speculate about what Altizer means. He seems to be using Kierkegaard's idea of dialectic or something very similar, which is Mircea Eliade's idea of the myth of the coincidence of opposites. If a person says yes to something with sufficient passion, this will somehow bring upon him the opposite. This means that if we fully affirm the profane and secular modern world, we will receive the sacred, a completely undeserved gift. For Altizer the sacred will be found only when Western man accepts the profane while desiring to change it.[15]

This coincidence of opposites would be like the highest expressions of mysticism as found in Oriental religions yet address itself to the historical destiny of contemporary man by transforming his profane world view into faith. This would be an eschatological faith because it calls man out of history, a meaningful course of events, into a new reality of grace. Oriental mysticism, Altizer explains, strikes the Western mind as following a way of radical world negation. But, like the highest religious expressions of both East and West, it is dialectical in that it denies this world to transform time into Eternity. It seeks to show this world as a veil upon an unfallen Totality.[16]

Viewing religion as a moving backward to an original sacredness, we can see that Christianity too is such a movement with its belief in a primordial God whose sacredness negates the profane and its expectation of an eschatological end which will be a return to the primordial beginning. But the uniqueness of Christianity does not lie here. Christianity is the only world religion to have occasioned a radically profane history. Christendom took the Incarnation to be the intersection of time and eternity, of flesh and spirit. In so doing, it gave up world negation for the new age of absolutely autonomous profane history.

The traditional image of the Incarnation made possible the sanctification of "time" and "nature." This led to the transformation of eternity into time. Christendom contains the willing of the death of God. From this we can gather that in God's fully becoming man in Christ and suffering death upon the cross God emptied himself, ceasing to be transcendent and simultaneously making himself present in the world. Thus, in dying, God makes himself present in the world, and he is thus partially or potentially present at every point in time and space. This we understand by knowing God's death in Christ.

The first thing to clear up about this view is exactly how one can claim that God is dead and at the same time try to speak in theological terms. Some readers have been over the early chapters of this book and witnessed the many attempts to prove God's existence through rational arguments, the defects of these arguments, and the rejection of these arguments even by people who would like to accept them. These readers will be puzzled and want to know how death-of-God theologians can now tell without any reflections on these arguments that God is dead. This decision comes more on the heels of the loss of emotional impact of the idea of God than on the heels of new philosophical considerations bearing against the existence of God. In other words, it may well be that there is no God-shaped emptiness in the heart of twentieth-century man, but this in itself should make no difference for the question, Does God exist?

These theologians, however, do not say "God does not exist"; they say "God is dead." The difference has to be that they believed God really did at one time exist. The trouble with this from the philosophical standpoint is that this belief can only be as good as the evidence for it, and we have seen that it is none too good. So the death-of-God move may be one corresponding to the morphology of belief in the sense that many of those who have believed in God no longer do and so God is dead for them. Still, it is nothing more than a poetic expression unless it is being held that God did really exist. And to hold this one brings down upon him all of the difficulties of traditional theism.

One cannot read much of the death-of-God theology without receiving the impression that it is suggesting a search for a new idea of God to replace the traditional one—to find an expression of the reality of God which is living for us in the modern world. This suggestion is far less radical and, in fact, is itself a very traditional idea, namely, that in any given age the image of God is always going to be the result of man's stretching his language, his concepts, and his imagination to express something none of these can fully express, and that as man's life changes these change, and with them the idea of God. But this interpretation is at most something one might discover along with much less radical ideas, and since it is so old it is far more interesting to look for the more radical interpretation of what the death-of-God theologians are saying. And, of course, even this old idea about man's image of God, no less than any of the new ideas, raises all of the philosophical questions about whether there really is a God.

A better interpretation of the idea of the death of God is as the loss of man's spiritual need for God. This, we have seen, is a major concern of death-of-God theology as it takes its rise from Bonhoeffer. Men no longer shape their institutions or act within them or in any other way conduct their lives in accordance with belief in God. There is no longer in men even the feeling of the loss of God. But without some way of showing men cannot get along well without God, or some way of showing or reason for hoping there is a God despite man's secular ways, there seems to be very little upon which to base a theology and every reason to get on with living the best secular life we know how to live.

With specific reference to Altizer, much depends upon his notion of the coincidence of opposites. This, I believe, is a very difficult notion—difficult to understand, but also, in a measure as it is understood, difficult to maintain. There is no reason, apart from belief in supernatural force, to believe that such an effect as the myth recounts ever occurs. And even the formulation of the death-of-God idea in dialectical terms has the difficulty mentioned earlier of including the idea that God at least did exist as well as the difficulty that it is at best one among many interpretations of the course of human events.

Finally, while this new theology does not make the common mistake of attributing the modern crisis of belief directly to the rise of science, it does seem to do it indirectly. For it not only accepts as its starting point modern man's refusal of religious belief, but it also accepts it as philosophically correct. This is to accept indirectly a philosophical view which holds that religious belief really is impossible. In recent decades the motivation for holding such a philosophical view has come from the very scientific orientation of the age. But it is by no means settled, and by no means clear what it would be to settle it, that the sciences answer all questions and are the basis of all belief, and the screen through which all questions and beliefs must pass in order to be judged legitimate. This is not to argue against such a philosophical position here but, rather, to call upon death-of-God theologians to offer a justification for acquiescing in the religious skepticism of our time. For they not only address themselves to it: they also share it. But this skepticism cannot readily be derived from the sciences themselves. It seems to come from the desire of men to understand themselves within a view somehow based solely on the sciences—whatever that would be.

An obvious point for the nonreligious person to raise is whether any religious view of man cannot be spelled out in a set of beliefs about man and his situation and submitted to rational scrutiny, resulting in the acceptance of those beliefs which are rationally tenable and the rejection of those which are not. And, more important, it will appear to the nonreligious man that the net result will be something we could have known without religion at all.

About all one can say on behalf of the religious man is that his view is not that sort of thing. In addition to the commitments he has to something more than the natural world, there are commitments to the entire scriptural experience in terms of which he sees himself and his world, and this cannot be spelled out in just so many propositions.

This is not just because the experience of the Bible which he chooses to make primary in his life is complex, but also because life is complex. There is no set of beliefs which can serve a man adequately without his supplementing, applying, or interpreting them and at the same time drawing on things he has learned and situations in which he has been and seen or read of others being in, and which show him strategies to apply or errors to avoid, so that he will bring forth something good from his situation.

Here we come upon the question of whether religion is a worthwhile way of life, whether there is any point in the religious life. Having already remarked that life is so exceedingly complex, when we stop to ask about ways of life it should be clear that we are rather near the limits of useful discussion. Some matters, even though they are quite properly philosophical, have to be dealt with by being put not to the test of reason or the test of experiment, but to the test of living. Unfortunately, a man has only one chance to make that test. Then, again, a long series of such tests could only be tedious. The demand we feel to make the most of the life we have can only make us realize what an adventure life is. The reflections on religion we have made in this book suggest rather strongly, I think, that religion is for making that adventure full and significant.

# Notes

## Chapter I

1. David Hume, *Dialogues Concerning Natural Religion*, ed. Henry D. Aiken (New York, 1948), p. 52.

2. There is a strong current of opinion today among theologians that Paley did not read Hume. For example, John Hick in his reader *The Existence of God*, pp. 103–4, says "Paley seems to be unaware of the devastating criticism Hume makes of the argument from design"; and Frederick Ferre in the otherwise very fine introduction to his edition of Paley's *Natural Theology* says "Amazing as it may appear, our author does not even refer to Hume by name in a period when, it may seem to us today, the only important task for philosophical thinkers was to wrestle with the challenging Scotsman." Hick and Ferre are simply mistaken. See Paley's reference to Hume in *Natural Theology* (Boston, 1831), Ch. XXVI, p. 315.

3. For an interesting discussion bearing on these considerations, see Alvin Plantinga, *God and Other Minds* (Ithaca, N.Y., 1967).

4. John Wisdom, *Philosophy and Psychoanalysis,* (Oxford, 1953), p. 149 ff.

5. See John Dewey, *A Common Faith* (New Haven, 1934), esp. 32 ff.

6. Hume, *Dialogues*, p. 66.

7. George Berkeley, *Principles of Human Knowledge* (La Salle, Ill., 1950), Part I, sect. 153.

8. For a discussion of this point, see John Hick, *Philosophy of Religion* (Englewood Cliffs, N.J., 1963), p. 40 ff.

9. Fyodor Dostoevsky, *The Brothers Karamazov*, trans. C. Garnett (New York, 1950), p. 288.

10. *Ibid.*, pp. 290–91.

11. Leo Tolstoy, "The Death of Ivan Ilych," trans. Aylmer Maude in *The Death of Ivan Ilyich and Other Stories* (New York, 1960), pp. 154–56.

12. T. S. Eliot, "The Cocktail Party," in *The Complete Poems and Plays* (New York, 1952), pp. 380–83.

### Chapter II

1. For reported instances, see Sir James Frazer, *The Golden Bough*, abridged ed. (New York, 1951), Ch. VII.

2. *Summa Contra Gentiles*, Bk. I, Ch. V.

3. *Ibid.*, Bk. I, Ch. VI.

4. *Ibid.*, Bk. I, Ch. VII, sect. 7.

5. John Locke, *An Essay Concerning Human Understanding*, ed. A. S. Pringle-Patterson (Oxford, 1924), Bk. IV, Ch. XVIII, p. 356.

6. *Ibid.*, Bk. IV, Ch. XVIII, sect. 5.

7. *Ibid.*, Bk. IV, Ch. XVIII, sect. 11.

8. *Summa Contra Gentiles*, Bk. I, Ch. VII, sect. 7.

9. Locke, Bk. IV, Ch. XVIII, sect. 10.

10. *Summa Theologica* I, Q. 68, Art. 3.

11. Emil Brunner, *Reason and Revelation*, tr. Olive Wyon (Philadelphia, 1946), p. 21.

12. Emil Brunner, *The Philosophy of Religion from the Standpoint of Protestant Theology*, tr. A. S. D. Farrer and B. L. Woolf (London, 1958), p. 420.

13. *Ibid.*, p. 169.

14. *Ibid.*, p. 109.

15. *Summa Theologica* I, Q. 1, Art. 10; *Ibid.*, I, Q. 1, Art. 1.

16. Sigmund Freud, *The Future of an Illusion*, tr. W. D. Robson-Scott (Garden City, N.Y., 1953), p. 44.

17. *Ibid.*, p. 45.

18. William Ralph Inge, *Lay Thoughts of a Dean* (Garden City, N.Y., 1926), p. 337 ff.

19. R. J. Zwi Werblowsky, "Miracle," *Encylopaedia Britannica*, XV, 1968.

20. *Ibid.*

21. See, for instance, *Milindapañha*, ed. V. Frenckner (London, 1880), 71.[16]

22. See, for instance, *Majjhima-Nikāya* (Sutta 63), ed. V. Frenckner (London, 1888).

23. Philostratus, *The Life of Apollonius of Tyana*, ed. F. C. Conybearer (Cambridge, Mass., 1927), I, pp. 457–59.

24. C. S. Lewis, *Miracles* (London, 1960), pp. 154–55.

25. *Summa Theologica* II, Q. 1, Art. 6.

26. David Hume, *An Enquiry Concerning Human Understanding*, ed. L. A. Selby-Bigge (Oxford, 1963), p. 109.

27. *Ibid.*, p. 114.

28. C. S. Lewis, *Miracles* (London, 1947), pp. 105–6.

29. *Ibid.*, p. 107.

30. Curt J. Ducasse, *Nature, Mind, and Death* (LaSalle, Ill., 1951), Ch. XIX.

31. George Santayana, *Three Philosophical Poets* (New York, 1938), pp. 51–53.

32. Nikos Kazantzakis, *Zorba the Greek*, tr. Carl Wildman (New York, 1965), p. 270.

33. Benedetto Croce, *My Philosophy* (New York, 1962), p. 239.

34. Geddes MacGregor, *Introduction to Religious Philosophy* (Boston, 1959), pp. 192–97.

## Chapter III

1. Hebrews 11:1.

2. C. N. Cochrane, *Christianity and Classical Culture* (New York, 1959), p. 402.

3. *Summa Theologica*, II, II. Q. 2, Art. 9.

4. *Confessions*, Bk. IV, Ch. X., tr. Edward B. Pusey D.D. (New York), p. 54.

5. *Ibid.*, Bk. VII, Ch. X.

6. See the section on Mysticism below.

7. Søren Kierkegaard, *Concluding Unscientific Postscript*, tr. David F. Swenson (Princeton, 1941), pp. 220–21.

8. *Ibid.*, p. 189.

9. *Ibid.*, p. 151.

10. See the section on Immortality above.

11. Kierkegaard, p. 178.

12. *Ibid.*, p. 178.

13. Harold Höffding, *Kierkegaard als Philosoph* (Stuttgart, 1896), p. 75.

14. George F. Thomas, *Religious Philosophies of the West* (New York, 1965), p. 316.

15. Kierkegaard, p. 182.

16. *Ibid.*, p. 182.

17. William P. Alston, *Religious Belief and Philosophical Thought* (New York, 1963), p. 434.

18. Kierkegaard, p. 188.

19. C. H. Jung, *Modern Man in Search of a Soul* (New York, 1933), p. 259.

20. See, for example, Rollo May, "The Origins and Significance of the Existential Movement in Psychology," in *Existence*, eds. Rollo May, Ernest Angel, and Henri F. Ellenberger (New York, 1958), esp. p. 8.

21. Martin Buber, *I and Thou* (New York, 1958), p. 34.

22. *Ibid.*, p. 34.

23. *Ibid.*, pp. 109–10.

24. Wilfrid Sellars, *Science, Perception and Reality* (New York, 1963), Chapter 1, "Philosophy and the Scientific Image of Man."

25. *Ibid.*, p. 9.

26. I Timothy 1:15.

27. Freud, p. 45.

28. *Ibid.*, p. 51.

29. *Ibid.*, pp. 55–56.

30. See also C. G. Jung, *Psychological Types* (New York, 1926).

31. J. F. Jacobi, *The Psychology of Jung* (New Haven, 1943), p. 8.

32. C. G. Jung, *Psychology and Religion* (New Haven, 1938), pp. 111–12.

33. *Ibid.*, p. 113–14.

34. *Ibid.*, p. 114.

35. *Ibid.*, p. 114.

## Chapter IV

1. See preceding chapter.

2. William James, *Varieties of Religious Experience* (New York, 1902), pp. 371–72.

3. C. B. Martin, *Religious Belief* (Ithaca, N.Y., 1959), esp. Chapter V.

4. See, for example, Rudolph Otto, *The Idea of the Holy*, tr. J. W. Harvey (Oxford, 1923).

5. St. Teresa of Avila, *Interior Castle*, tr. the Benedictines of Stanbrook. Rev. the Very Reverend Prior Zimmerman, O.C.D. (London, 1930), p. 171.

6. John Hick, *Faith and Knowledge* (Ithaca, N.Y., 1957), p. 110.

7. *Ibid.*, p. 120.

8. *Ibid.*, pp. 127–28.

9. Walter T. Stace, "What is Mysticism?" in *The Teachings of the Mystics*, ed. Walter T. Stace (New York, 1960), pp. 9–29.

10. Evelyn Underhill, *Mysticism* (New York, 1961), p. 79.

11. Stace, pp. 22–23.

12. Bertrand Russell, *Religion and Science* (New York, 1935), pp. 187–88.

13. *Ibid.*, p. 188.

14. A. J. Ayer, *Language, Truth, and Logic* (New York, 1946), pp. 115, 117, quoted by Max Black in *The Labyrinth of Language* (New York, 1970).

15. See Gilbert Ryle, "The Verification Principle," *Révue Internationale de Philosophie*, Vol. 5, 1951, p. 250.

16. See Anthony Flew, "Theology and Falsifications" (A), in *New Essays in Philosophical Theology*, eds. Anthony Flew and Alasdair MacIntyre (London, 1955), pp. 96–99.

17. *Ibid.*, p. 99.

18. R. M. Hare, "Theology and Falsification" (B), in Flew and Mac-Intyre, pp. 99–103.

19. Basil Mitchell, "Theology and Falsification" (C), in Flew and Mac-Intyre, pp.103–5.

20. I. M. Crombie, "Theology and Falsification" (E), in Flew and MacIntyre, p. 118.

21. *Ibid.*, pp. 124–25.

## Chapter V

1. Fyodor Dostoevsky, *Notes From the Underground*, tr. Andrew R. MacAndrew (New York, 1961), pp. 98–99.

2. Alfred North Whitehead, *Science and the Modern World* (New York, 1925), pp. 13–14.

3. Kurt Baier, "The Meaning of Life" in *Twentieth Century Philosophy: The Analytic Tradition*, ed. Morris Weitz (New York, 1966), pp. 361–79.

4. Leo Tolstoy, "A Confession" in *A Confession, The Gospel in Brief, and What I Believe*, tr. Aylmer Maude (London, 1940), pp. 15–16.

5. *Ibid.*, p. 16.

6. Albert Camus, *The Myth of Sisyphus*, tr. Justin O'Brien (New York, 1960), pp. 22–23.

7. *Ibid.*, p. 37.

8. D. T. Suzuki, *Essays in Zen Buddism: First Series* (New York, 1927).

9. Quoted by D. T. Suzuki, *op. cit.*

10. Quoted by John B. Noss, *Man's Religions* (New York, 1963), p. 236.

11. *Ibid.*, p. 236.

12. Thomas J. J. Altizer and William Hamilton, *Radical Theology and the Death of God* (New York, 1966), Preface.

13. Dietrich Bonhoeffer, *Letters and Papers from Prison*, tr. Reginald H. Fuller, ed. Eberhard Bethage (New York, 1953), pp. 162–63.

14. Quoted in Altizer and Hamilton, p. 104.

15. Altizer and Hamilton, p. 29.

16. Thomas J. J. Altizer, *The Gospel of Christian Atheism* (Philadelphia, 1966), p. 37.

# Supplementary
# Bibliography

Braithwaite, R. B., *An Empiricist's View of the Nature of Religious Experience* (Cambridge: Cambridge University Press, 1955).

Buber, Martin, *The Writings of Martin Buber,* selected by W. Herberg (New York: Meridian Books, 1956).

Bultmann, Rudolf, *Essays Philosophical and Theological,* tr. Greig (New York: Macmillan, 1955).

Burtt, Edwin A., *The Metaphysical Foundation of Modern Science,* rev. ed. (New York: Harcourt Brace, 1932).

Bury, John, *The Idea of Progress* (New York: Macmillan, 1932).

Casserley, Julian Victor Langmead, *The Christian in Philosophy* (London: Faber and Faber, 1949).

Collingwood, R. G., *Faith and Reason,* ed. Lionel Rubinoff (Chicago: Quandrangle, 1968).

———, *Speculum Mentis* (Oxford: Oxford University Press, 1924).

Durkheim, Emile, *The Elementary Forms of the Religious Life* (New York: Macmillan, 1915).

Hepburn, Ronald W., *Christianity and Paradox* (London: Watts, 1958).

Hook, Sidney, ed., *Religious Experience and Truth* (New York: New York University Press, 1961).

Kant, Immanuel, *Religion within the Limits of Reason Alone* (LaSalle: Open Court, 1934).

Kaufmann, Walter Arnold, *Critique of Religion and Philosophy* (New York: Harper, 1958).

Kierkegaard, Søren Aaby, *Attack upon Christendom,* tr. Lowry (Princeton: Princeton University Press, 1944).

————, *Fear and Trembling* and *The Sickness unto Death* (New York: Doubleday, Anchor Books, 1954).

————, *Philosophical Fragments,* tr. Swenson (Princeton: Princeton University Press, 1936).

Lamont, Corliss, *Humanism as a Philosophy* (New York: Philosophical Library, 1949).

Lewis, Clive Stapes, *Mere Christianity* (New York: Macmillan, 1956).

————, *The Problem of Pain* (New York: Macmillan, 1943).

————, *The Screwtape Letters* (New York: Macmillan, 1944).

MacGregor, Geddes, *Aesthetic Experience in Religion* (London: Macmillan, 1947).

Macquarrie, John, *An Existentialist Theology* (New York: Macmillan, 1955).

————, *Principles of Christian Theology* (New York: Scribner, 1966).

Mascall, E. L., *Christian Theology and Natural Science* (New York: Ronald Press, 1956).

————, *Existence and Analogy* (New York: Longmans, Green, 1949).

Matthews, W. R., *God in Christian Thought and Experience* (London: Nisbet, 1930).

Mitchell, Basil, ed., *Faith and Logic* (Boston: Beacon Press, 1957).

Niebuhr, Helmut Richard, *The Meaning of Revelation* (New York: Macmillan, 1942).

Niebuhr, Reinhold, *Does Civilization Need Religion?* (New York: Macmillan, 1927).

————, *Faith and History* (New York: Scribner, 1949).

————, *The Nature and Destiny of Man* (2 vols.: Vol. 1, *Human Nature;* Vol. 2, *Human Destiny*) (New York: Scribner, 1941–43).

Paton, Herbert James, *The Modern Predicament* (New York: Macmillan, 1955).

Ramsay, Ian T., *Religious Language* (London: A. R. Allenson, 1957).

Religion in America, *Daedelus,* Vol. 96, No. 1: Winter 1967.

Russell, Bertrand, *Why I Am Not a Christian* (New York: Simon and Schuster, 1957).

Santoni, Ronald E., ed., *Religious Language and the Problem of Religious Knowledge* (Bloomington: Indiana University Press, 1968).

Smart, N., *Reasons and Faiths:* an investigation of religious discourse, Christian and non-Christian (London: Routledge & Kegan Paul, 1958).

————, *A Dialogue of Religions* (London: S.C.M. Press, 1960).

————, *Historical Selections in the Philosophy of Religion* (London: S.C.M. Press, 1962).

Sorley, W. F., *Moral Values and the Idea of God* (Cambridge: Cambridge University Press, 1919).

Stace, Walter Terence, *Religion and the Modern Mind* (Philadelphia: Lippincott, 1952).

Taylor, A. E., *Does God Exist?* (New York: Macmillan, 1947).

Tennant, F. R., *Philosophical Theology,* 2 vols. (Cambridge: Cambridge University Press, 1928–30).

Tillich, Paul Johannes, *Systematic Theology,* 2 vols. (Chicago: University of Chicago Press, 1951–57).

Whitehead, Alfred North, *Religion in the Making* (New York: Macmillan, 1926).

Zaehner, R. C., *Mysticism Sacred and Profane* (Oxford: Clarendon Press, 1957).

# Index